jim burns

general editor

uncommon object lessons and discussion starters

leader's resource

Published by Gospel Light

Ventura, California, U.S.A.

www.gospellight.com

Printed in the U.S.A.

Previously published in the Fresh Ideas series as *Case Studies, Talk Sheets and Discussion Starters* (compiled by Mark Simone) published in 1997 and *Hot Topics* (Jim Burns and Mike DeVries, general editors) in 2002.

Library of Congress Cataloging-in-Publication Data
Case studies, talk sheets, and discussion starters.
Uncommon object lessons & discussion starters / Jim Burns, general editor.
p. cm.
First work originally published: Case studies, talk sheets, and discussion starters. [S.l. : s.n.], 1997. (Fresh ideas series).
2nd work originally published: Hot topics. [S.l. : s.n.], 2002.
Includes bibliographical references and index.
ISBN 978-0-8307-5098-6 (trade paper : alk. paper)
1. Christian education of young people. 2. Object-teaching. I. Burns, Jim, 1953- II. Title.
III. Title: Uncommon object lessons and discussion starters. IV. Title: Hot topics.
BV1485.C25 2010
259'.23—dc22
2009054206

All definitions are from the Merriam-Webster online dictionary.
http://www.merriam-webster.com.

1 2 3 4 5 6 7 8 9 10 11 12 13 14 15 / 16 15 14 13 12 11 10

Rights for publishing this book outside the U.S.A. or in non-English languages are administered by Gospel Light Worldwide, an international not-for-profit ministry. For additional information, please visit www.glww.org, email info@glww.org, or write to Gospel Light Worldwide, 1957 Eastman Avenue, Ventura, CA 93003, U.S.A.

This book is dedicated to **Todd Dean***.*
Thank you for your friendship and years of leadership with YouthBuilders and HomeWord. Daily we are reaching people at HomeWord because of your skill and effort. You are a blessing in my life.

Jim Burns

contents

sin & confession

spiritual growth

discussion starters

Christian living

handling conflict

hardships & suffering

helping others

integrity

peer pressure & sexuality

racism & prejudice

responsibility

salvation & faith

you be the judge

indexes

introduction

I hope you will love this book as much as I do! As a youth worker and the general editor of this project, I know how beneficial it is to get students talking and discussing the important issues of their lives. I think you will agree that this book has a little something for everybody when it comes to getting your students to open up and talk.

Edgar Dale, one of the great educators of the last century, informs us that when students are spoken or written to their retention level is only 5 to 10 percent, but when they are active participants in experiential learning, the retention can be expanded to as much as 85 percent. That's why this book is so important. Students learn best when *they talk*, not when *we talk at them*.

Over the years, I've often noticed that the best meetings with the most energy are always the ones with interaction and discussion. Participation seems to be the ingredient for a successful youth meeting. When someone talks at the students, the success of the meeting is dependent on the speaker being dynamic or on the subject hitting the mark. When there is group interaction and discussion, however, the meeting works almost every time.

The good news is that you do not need to be a gifted speaker to affect the learning and spiritual growth of your students. Instead, you can become a good facilitator of communication and interaction among your students. This resource book will show you how. In putting together the material for this book, Mark Simone and I asked youth workers from the front lines to send us their best stuff for getting students to think and talk about the important real-life issues of living out their Christianity. Within these pages you will find object lessons taken directly out of real situations and other types of discussion starters that have already been used successfully with students. You'll be introduced to a wonderful style of teaching and learning that encourages thought-provoking discussions.

Our goal as Christian youth workers and teachers of adolescents is to plant God's Word in students' lives and to help them actively live out their faith. Oftentimes, using the kinds of experiences in this book will do a better and more effective job than any sermon or youth talk. A discussion in which the students discover the truth for themselves with your guidance can be a powerful tool for active learning.

God bless you as you help youth navigate through the not-so-easy world of adolescence. Thanks for being a difference-maker and for being committed to youth.

Jim Burns
San Juan Capistrano, California

OBJECT LESSONS

object lesson \ ab-jikt le-sen \ **1a:** a concrete illustration of a moral or principle **1b:** a lesson taught by using a material object **2:** something that serves as a practical example of a principle or abstract idea.

Object lessons are great. In my first youth ministry job after I graduated from seminary, I often gave the children's sermon at our church. I would usually use a fun object lesson to bring home a point the children could understand. I was always amazed that after the service many adults would come up to me and comment on the object lesson. I still remember the time one of the older members in our congregation enthusiastically told me, "It finally makes sense. When you brought out the little duckie and explained the Trinity, it finally made sense!" That day, I was reminded that even adults learn best with object lessons—even if you use a little duckie to get the point across. ☺

1

any light makes a difference

key verses

"You are the light of the world. A city on a hill cannot be hidden. Neither do people light a lamp and put it under a bowl. Instead they put it on its stand, and it gives light to everyone in the house. In the same way, let your light shine before men, that they may see your good deeds and praise your Father in heaven" (Matthew 5:14-16).

materials needed

small flashlight
large battery-powered lantern
small penlight or candle for each person
a few lighters (if you use the candles)
a box large enough to cover the lantern

preparation

Gather all of the items together and turn out the lights in the room.

object lesson

As the group sits in the darkness, explain that in Matthew 5:14-16, Jesus taught that Christians are like lights set on a hill and that the light would be no good if it were hidden. Use the different lights to illustrate the following points about light and Christians as lights in a dark world:

- *One small flashlight*: Even a small light in darkness will make a difference. There is no Christian who is less important or has less to do. All light, no matter the size, will shatter the darkness.

- *The large lantern and the box*: This large lantern will drastically change the darkness. But if you put a box or blanket over it, it cannot be seen. If we hide our light, it will have no effect on the dark world.

- *The penlights (or candles)*: Hand these out to the group but instruct them not to turn them on yet. If you are using penlights, click one on and then walk around the room touching the other penlights. Each time you touch a student's penlight, have him or her click it on. If you use candles, walk around with a lighter and light the candles one at a time. Explain how one light lighting another light brightens the world.

Ask your group how Christians can hide Christ's light. Have students give an example of a Christian they know who shines and gives light to everyone around. Challenge them to think of ways they can be a light in the darkness on their school campus during the next week.

additional scriptures

John 1:3-5; 3:19-21; 8:12; 12:46; Acts 13:47; Romans 13:12; 2 Corinthians 4:6; Ephesians 5:8-14; 1 John 2:9-11

2

shattering sin

key verse

"Anyone who does not take his cross and follow me is not worthy of me" (Matthew 10:38).

materials needed

lots of coins
a glass jar with a screw-on lid
several pillows or cushions
a tarp
index cards
pens or pencils

preparation

Put the coins in a pint-sized mayonnaise or similar jar (one with a top that screws on tightly). Have a good mix of several different sizes of coins, and also have a wide pile of pillows ready, stacked deep. You will be tossing the jar on the pillows, so make sure it's deep enough. Also set up a tarp in an area where you will be shattering the jar. Place this area far enough away from the students to ensure their safety when you break the jar.

object lesson

Explain that there are certain things that all human beings need, and then ask the group to call out what some of those needs are (for example, air, water, food, love, sense of belonging, the forgiveness of sins, a relationship with God, peace). Give a few volunteers the index cards and the pens or pencils. As the needs are suggested, have the volunteers write them down on the index cards and put them on the pillows.

Next, display the jar of coins and explain to the group that the coins represent God's desire to provide for the needs of all humans. Drop the jar on the pillows and remark that God's answers are not getting through to the needs of people because their hearts have become encased in the hard glass jar of human sin. Then, with the volunteers' help, move the needs cards to the tarp and have everyone stand back a good distance. Drop the jar on the tarp, allowing it to shatter. (*Note*: Be sure not to throw the jar down, as this may result in shards of glass spraying up from the tarp.)

Discuss how being "soft" Christians who present a soft gospel can deceive people into thinking they can accept the Lord and then go do whatever they want. We need to present the hard truths of the gospel and the promise that Christ changes lives and forgives sins. Talk about the difference between a soft gospel that makes it sound easy to follow Jesus and makes people think that anyone can be a believer on his or her own terms and the true gospel that tells about our sin, our need for a Savior, and the fact that we must deny ourselves, pick up our crosses daily and follow Him.

Suggest that Christians are like the shattered mayonnaise jar. We need to be broken by the impact of our own sin before we can have any effect on the world around us. Challenge students to become devoted to the truth and to live their relationship with God before a lost and hurting world.

To conclude the lesson, discuss some examples of Christians being too soft and watering down the gospel. Ask students what the gospel of Jesus is and why living Christ's way is so important. Discuss how you, as a youth group, can be more straightforward in your faith by meeting just one of the needs that the group discussed. Challenge students to choose a need that was suggested and then plan a way, as a group, of meeting that need.

additional scriptures

Psalm 86:11; Matthew 25:31-45; Luke 9:23-26; 14:25-35

3

when candles burn out

key verse

"No one lights a lamp and hides it in a jar or puts it under a bed. Instead, he puts it on a stand, so that those who come in can see the light" (Luke 8:16).

materials needed

a package of birthday candles and one larger candle
candleholders and clay
lighters or matches
blankets/towels

preparation

Before the meeting, time how long it will take for either a few small candles or a bunch of birthday candles to burn out. You will be talking in sync with the candles burning out for this object lesson, so you will need to know how much time you have. Hold the meeting in a room that can be entirely darkened, even stuffing blankets and/or towels around doors and windows to keep light from creeping in. Also turn out the lights in adjacent rooms.

object lesson

Gather students in the darkened meeting room and light the birthday candles as the only source of illumination. Stick the candles in clay inside glass or metal candleholders, place them in the corners of the room, and have adult leaders light them simultaneously.

Begin the lesson by explaining that we as believers in Christ are His lights in a darkened world and that each of us, combined with the whole Body of Christ, keeps the darkness at bay. Read the key verse in Luke 8:16 and some of the additional Scriptures listed below while the candles burn lower. As the candles begin to sputter out, shift the talk to focus on those who don't know God and, more importantly, those who reject God.

When the darkness is complete, ask the students to get up and to slowly move about the room. Have the adult advisors quickly set some obstacles in the way, such as sections of cardboard, plastic or even dry cereal that will crunch when stepped on. Also have the advisors quickly set up a few chairs for them to bump into. (*Note*: To avoid injuries, warn students to move slowly and not push. Ask them to simply move to another location in the room and sit down.)

At the conclusion of the object lesson, light the larger candle and note to the group how it fills up the darkness in the room with light. Then ask the students what it was like to see the candles beginning to go out and to be gradually surrounded by darkness. Ask how they felt when they moved around in the dark room and what steps they took to protect themselves as they moved about. Finally, discuss how they felt when the larger candle was lit and the darkness was dispelled.

additional scriptures

2 Samuel 22:29; Psalms 18:28; 19:8; 27:1; 89:15; 119:105,130; Proverbs 4:18-19; Isaiah 9:2; 60:1-3,19-20; Micah 7:8-9; Matthew 4:16; 6:22-23; John 1:4-5,9; 3:19-21; 8:12; 12:46; Romans 13:12; 2 Corinthians 4:6; Ephesians 5:8-14; 1 Thessalonians 5:4-6; 1 Peter 2:9; 1 John 1:5-7; 2:8-11

4

bruised on the inside

key verse

"Carry each other's burdens, and in this way you will fulfill the law of Christ" (Galatians 6:2).

materials needed

two bananas

preparation

Just before presenting the lesson, carefully mash the insides of one of the bananas without breaking the peel. The goal is to bruise the insides of one banana while keeping both bananas looking the same outside. This will demonstrate that though the bananas may look the same on the outside, they are radically different on the inside.

object lesson

Show the two bananas, noting that they look pretty much the same—they both look like they taste good and would be a great snack. Open the good banana and show it to the students. Then open the bruised banana and show that it is badly bruised on the inside, even though it looks fine on the outside.

Share the key verse in Galatians 6:2. Explain that most people do a good job of looking as though everything is going okay in their lives, but the reality is that many are hurting. As Christians, we are called to carry one another's burdens and come alongside each other for encouragement and support. Through building and deepening relationships with one another, we are able to see what is really going on in each other's lives and effectively care for one another.

Conclude the lesson by discussing with the group how they can identify when someone is hurting. What are the signs they look for? Ask them to think of some ways that they can fulfill the command to "carry each other's burdens." Discuss how encouraging another person can help that person face a difficult situation. Finally, have students share how someone has encouraged them when they were feeling bruised or overburdened.

additional scriptures

Ecclesiastes 4:9-12; John 15:12; Romans 1:12; 15:1-2; 1 Corinthians 12:26; Ephesians 4:29; 1 Thessalonians 3:2-3; Hebrews 3:13; 10:25; James 5:16

5

a candle in the dark

key verses

"Let us consider how we may spur one another on toward love and good deeds. Let us not give up meeting together, as some are in the habit of doing, but let us encourage one another" (Hebrews 10:24-25).

materials needed

utility candles (enough for every group member to have his or her own)
small paper plates (with a hole in the middle of each plate)
matches

object lesson

As group members arrive, hand a candle and a small paper plate to each person. Have everyone sit in a circle. Instruct the group members to slip the bottom of their candles into the hole in the middle of the plate. (*A word of caution*: Check with fire and safety codes before you do this activity inside a building.)

Next, state, "We live in a world that is without much hope. Everywhere you turn there seem to be people living without hope. In Ephesians 4:17-19, Paul says that our world is filled with darkness. Our calling as Christians is to shine out hope in the midst of our dark world. One way we can do that is through encouraging one another."

Read the key verse in Hebrews 10:24-25 and then say, "Tonight, we're going to live out this verse by shining out the light and hope of encouragement to one another." Light your candle, and then turn out the lights. Ask everyone to stand up and stay in the circle. Select one person in the group, walk to that person, and tell him or her one encouraging thing while lighting his or her candle.

After you have lighted the first candle, have that person do the same to another person in the room. Continue until everyone in the room has their candles lighted. When this is accomplished, comment about how one light passed along to another eventually illuminated the whole room. You might want to end this time of encouragement by singing a praise song or with a time of prayer. Have students blow out their candles, and then turn on the lights before continuing.

Next, read John 13:34-35 and spend some time talking about the power of encouragement in our lives as well as bringing light into a dark world. Say, "In a real sense, when we encourage those around us, we are being a light in our darkened world. We are showing that we are followers of God."

Have students keep their (unlit) candles as a reminder to be a light in their world through the power of encouragement.

additional scriptures

Proverbs 18:21; Matthew 5:14-16; 12:34-37; John 13:34-35; Ephesians 4:29-32; 5:8-9

6

the words we speak

key verse

"Do not let any unwholesome talk come out of your mouths, but only what is helpful for building others up according to their needs, that it may benefit those who listen" (Ephesians 4:29).

materials needed

a trashcan filled with trash (the dirtier and smellier the better)
a mirror
a gift-wrapped box

object lesson

Hold up the trashcan, then the mirror, and then finally the gift-wrapped box. As you hold up each item, ask the group, "How does this item represent the words that we speak?" Allow students time to respond before going on to the next item. When they make their responses, ask them to clarify and give examples or Scriptures that might help them explain their insight.

After each item has been discussed (or after you have held up and discussed all three), explain the following insights:

The trashcan: Sometimes our words are filthy, just like this filthy trash can. No one wants to be around us. Sometimes the words that we speak are as useless as garbage in building others up.

The mirror: Our words reflect what's in our hearts—whether good or bad. Our words can reflect what God thinks about a person. Our words can show someone what is inside of them, even if they don't see it. Our words reflect the level of our relationship with God.

The gift: Our words can be a gift of encouragement in the lives of others. Just as people treasure certain gifts, our words can be treasures in people's hearts—things they will hold on to when they are discouraged or lonely. Our words can bring a smile to someone's day. Our words of encouragement are a gift of God to others.

additional scriptures

Proverbs 18:21; Matthew 12:34-37; 15:10-11,18; Luke 6:43-45; Ephesians 5:4; Colossians 3:8; Hebrews 3:12-13; 10:24-25; James 1:19-21,26; 3:1-12

7

follow the manual

key verses

"All Scripture is God-breathed and is useful for teaching, rebuking, correcting and training in righteousness, so that the man of God may be thoroughly equipped for every good work" (2 Timothy 3:16-17).

materials needed

a small, unassembled item (such as an appliance or a model) that has a lot of parts

an instructional manual (for how to put the item together)

object lesson

Display the unassembled item, showing the large number of parts. Explain how there are two options for assembling this item. The first option is to ignore the instruction manual and just hope for the best as you begin assembling the parts. The second option is to use the instruction manual and follow its guidance for assembling the item. (*Option*: If you have time, have two groups try to assemble identical items, but give only one group the instructions.)

Share the key verse in 2 Timothy 3:16-17. Explain that some people choose to assemble items without first consulting the instruction manual. Sometimes this works out for them and the item functions as it was intended to function, but at other times their disregard for the instructions leads to the item not functioning or to parts being left out that are needed to make the item operate properly.

State that it is the same with our lives. Too often we ignore the Bible—our instruction manual for living—and think we know how to put our lives together. Sometimes we can get along for a while without too much trouble, but eventually, if we ignore the Bible's instructions for our lives, we will run into difficulties. Our lives don't seem to work right. We make mistakes and our sin causes problems. In order to make sure that we live our lives the way God intended, we need to regularly read and study God's Word.

Discuss with the group what 2 Timothy 3:16 states is the purpose for us studying Scripture. Ask the students why they think so many Christians struggle to read the Bible on a regular basis if it is truly God's instruction manual for living. Have them share their number-one reason for not reading and studying the Bible more often and ask what they would be willing to change in order to spend more time reading and studying God's Word.

additional scriptures

Psalm 119:1-3,9-11,24,35,89-93,97-105,133; 1 Thessalonians 2:13; Hebrews 4:12-13; 2 Peter 1:3-4

8

the power of soap

key verse

"Be careful to obey all the law my servant Moses gave you; do not turn from it to the right or to the left, that you may be successful wherever you go" (Joshua 1:7).

materials needed

a bar of soap still sealed in the original box or wrapper

object lesson

Hold up the bar of soap still in its box. Ask the question, "How is God's Word like this bar of soap?" Allow the group to discuss for a few minutes.

Tell the group, "This soap has the power to clean you and remove dirt from your body. Inside this box [or wrapper] is a bar that contains the chemicals needed to clean your body. But as long as the bar is in this box [or wrapper], the chemicals are useless. For you to release the power of the soap, you need to take the bar out of the box and apply it to your body."

Continue by stating, "God's Word is exactly like this. It has the power to transform your life. It has the power to change your life completely, but as long as it sits unopened, that power can never be released. God's Word is living and active, but to release its power you first need to apply it. To release the power of God's Word, you need to open it up, read it, and—most importantly—use it in your life. Soap is faithful to accomplish its purpose when properly applied, just as is God's Word."

additional scriptures

Psalms 1; 119:9-16,97,105-112; Proverbs 8:32-35; John 1:1,14; 15:9-11; 17:16-17; Romans 15:4; Hebrews 4:12; James 1:22-25; 1 Peter 2:2

9

worthless!

key verses

"But he knows the way that I take; when he has tested me, I will come forth as gold. My feet have closely followed his steps; I have kept to his way without turning aside. I have not departed from the commands of his lips; I have treasured the words of his mouth more than my daily bread" (Job 23:10-12).

materials needed

a street map (which will be destroyed)
a Bible

object lesson

Begin the object lesson by holding up that map. Ask the students what the map is used for and allow them some time to respond. Then say something like, "A map is used for guidance. When we want to reach an unfamiliar destination, we check out the map. It tells us what we need to know so that we can reach our destination."

Now hold up the Bible. Explain that the Bible is just like a map—a map that God has given us that will guide us through all the crossroads and intersections of life. If we are wise, we will get to know the Bible. We will read it, learn what it says and, most important, follow its instructions.

Read the key verses in Job 23:10-12. Explain that in this passage, Job was comparing his relationship with God to a path on which he walked. State that Job was a wise man because he obviously followed God's map. Now say, "Some Christians foolishly do not read or obey the Word of God. They ignore the Bible—and eventually they suffer for their foolishness by becoming mixed up and confused." As you say this, begin to tear parts of the map off and drop them to the floor.

Hold up the torn map and explain that just as this map is now nearly useless, an unread Bible is not going to help anyone. Encourage the group members to read their Bibles and to remember the words of Colossians 3:16: "Let the word of Christ dwell in you richly." Explain that this means they are to fill their heads and hearts with the Bible. If any of the students

are finding the Bible hard to understand, offer to talk with them and help them find portions of the Bible that are easier to read and understand.

Conclude the lesson by reminding the group that God gave us His Word to help guide us through the problems of life. However, to get that instruction, we have to read it and follow it.

additional scriptures

Romans 10:8; Colossians 3:16; Hebrews 4:12; 2 Timothy 3:16

10

walk by the Spirit

key verse

"But I say, walk by the Spirit, and you will not carry out the desire of the flesh" (Galatians 5:16, *NASB*).

materials needed

a shoe

object lesson

Take off one of your shoes and show it to your students (you can make a humorous reference to the smell, if you like). Ask the group, "What is the purpose of a shoe?" Allow students to respond, and then say something like, "A shoe is meant to protect the foot as it moves across the bumps and sharp objects of this world. A shoe can also make a nice fashion statement. In addition, some shoes are designed to keep our feet warm, while others can help us in certain sports, like football or basketball. Sometimes, shoes can be a disadvantage, like when we try to swim. But whatever the case, shoes are primarily meant to help us walk and run in comfort."

Read the key verse in Galatians 5:16 to your students. Explain to the students that this verse contains God's instructions on how we as Christians are to walk in this world: "By the Spirit." Explain that this means we are to do what God says, follow Him, and go where He goes. We are to stay on the path He sets for us, not walk away to the right or left.

Note to the group that this verse also contains a promise: that if we walk by the Spirit, we won't carry out the desire of the flesh. This means that as we walk in God's ways, we will tend to become less and less tangled in sin. A person who doesn't walk by the Spirit will trip over the sins of this world, just like a person without shoes will stub his toes and bruise his soles. But a person who walks by the Spirit will get where he's going without injury.

Conclude by stating that in order to be the man or woman that God wants us to be, we have to walk by the Spirit. We need to trust and follow God and believe that He will see us through to the very end.

additional scriptures

Matthew 11:28-30; John 10:27; Romans 8:1-14; 2 Corinthians 7:1

11

the wedding ring

key verses

"And you also were included in Christ when you heard the word of truth, the gospel of your salvation. Having believed, you were marked in him with a seal, the promised Holy Spirit, who is a deposit guaranteeing our inheritance until the redemption of those who are God's possession—to the praise of his glory" (Ephesians 1:13-14).

materials needed

wedding ring (or a ring that looks like a real wedding ring)

object lesson

Show everyone the ring (pass it around, if you like), and say something like this: "In olden days, a king would wear a signet ring—a ring that had the king's emblem carved on it. When the king would send an official letter or document, he would seal the letter with wax. The emblem on the ring would be pressed into the hot wax to prove that this was a genuine document from the king. Today, people who are joined in marriage wear wedding rings as a seal or symbol of their partnership and commitment. The ring proclaims that the marriage is real and the partnership is genuine."

Now read the key verses in Ephesians 1:13-14. Ask the group to carefully consider what this passage says: A person who has received salvation has also received the Holy Spirit as a seal and a deposit guaranteeing his or her inheritance—eternal life. State that in the days when this was written, a seal was used to prove ownership. The fact that the Holy Spirit has been given to us proves that we belong to God. We are committed to Him and He is committed to us—just like two people who are married. However, unlike many marriages that fall apart, our seal with the Holy Spirit will never be broken. It is a partnership that will last forever.

additional scriptures

Acts 1:8; 5:32; Romans 5:3-5; 8:1-27; 1 Corinthians 3:16; 1 Thessalonians 1:5-6

12

the apple cart

key verse

"For there is no difference between Jew and Gentile—the same Lord is Lord of all and richly blesses all who call on him" (Romans 10:12).

materials needed

a plastic toy wheelbarrow
a variety of apples (Granny Smith, Red Delicious and Fuji)

preparation

Layer the apples in the wheelbarrow, making sure to keep each with its own kind.

object lesson

As the meeting begins, point out the wheelbarrow. Then point out the three different types of apples in the wheelbarrow and highlight the differences not only in color but also in taste, texture, uses (e.g., some are better suited for baking) and region in which they are grown.

Pick up one of each of the varieties and explain that as unique as each variety may be, every one of these is still an apple. Ask, "How are people similar to these apples?" Allow for responses, and then state, "We are all unique; each one of us has something that is different from anyone else in the world. When someone uses these differences as an excuse to dislike—and sometimes even hate—others, it's called prejudice. Prejudice is judging others based on what can be seen with our eyes and not bothering to find out who they really are inside."

Ask volunteers to share about their own experience or the experience of someone they've known who has been the target of prejudice. Allow for several responses, and then ask a volunteer to read Romans 10:12. Conclude by asking, "What does this verse tell us about God's view of prejudice? Why do we make distinctions between ourselves and others?"

additional scriptures

2 Corinthians 5:17-21; Galatians 3:26-29; Ephesians 2:10; Colossians 3:11-17

13

faulty first impressions

key verse

"But the Lord said to Samuel, 'Do not consider his appearance or his height, for I have rejected him. The Lord does not look at the things man looks at. Man looks at the outward appearance, but the Lord looks at the heart'" (1 Samuel 16:7).

materials needed

a (clean!) litter box
a cat litter pooper-scooper (also clean)
boxes of Grape Nuts
six thick, stubby Tootsie Rolls

preparation

This object lesson works best in a home setting. Done correctly, it is also one that your students will never forget. Before the lesson, fill the litter box about half full with Grape Nuts. Next, microwave the Tootsie Rolls until they become soft enough to mold into the shape of . . . well . . . let's just call them "litter box snacks." For added effect, while the shaped Tootsie Rolls are still warm, roll them around in the Grape Nuts to get some of the cereal to stick. Then place the shaped Tootsie Rolls in strategic places in the litter box, with some buried and some sticking up above the Grape Nuts. The goal here is to make it look like a real, well-used litter box.

object lesson

Bring out the litter box for the lesson. Tell the students that they all, of course, know what this object is. Using the pooper-scooper, fish out a Tootsie Roll and hold it with the scooper for the students to see. Ask those in the group how much they would pay for you to take a bite of the "litter-box snack." Go ahead and take the challenge. You should get quite a reaction from the group.

(*Note*: Some students may literally start gagging here, so work quickly before you lose your audience. If you think that this will be too gross for you or your group, you can do a similar object lesson using a potted plant that has been placed in soil made of crushed Oreo cookies. At the appropriate time in the lesson, eat the Oreo dirt.)

After you've had your little snack, share the key verse from 1 Samuel 16:7. Explain to the group that what you just ate was actually a Tootsie Roll, and that they all jumped to the wrong conclusion. Some things are not what they appear to be at first glance! In the same way, we often make judgments about people based on first impressions. However, we should beware when doing this, because some people are not what they seem to be at first.

Continue by stating that all too often we make judgments about others based on characteristics that aren't really important. For instance, we might make judgments based on a person's physical appearance, clothing, or how outgoing, intelligent or funny he or she is. But these outward signs may not be a true picture of a person's real self. Explain that God values each person because He created each one of us. He never makes a judgment based on outward appearances. He values us for who we really are on the inside. So the next time you are tempted to jump to a conclusion about a person because of a poor first impression, remember the Litter-Box snack lesson and look at others through God's eyes.

Conclude the lesson by asking students to give an example of a time when they made a mistake in judging someone based on first impressions. What changed their mind? Ask if they have had a similar experience in which someone judged them by a first impression. If so, what happened when that person got to know them better? Finally, discuss the dangers of making an incorrect judgment about someone based on first impressions and talk about how 1 Samuel 16:7 states we should judge others.

additional scriptures

Isaiah 53:2-12; Matthew 7:1-5; John 7:24; Romans 14:9-12; 15:7; Galatians 2:6; James 2:1-12; 4:12

14

commitment is costly

key verses

"If anyone would come after me, he must deny himself and take up his cross daily and follow me. For whoever wants to save his life will lose it, but whoever loses his life for me will save it" (Luke 9:23-24).

materials needed

egg
piece of ham or bacon

object lesson

Hold the egg in one hand and the ham or bacon in the other. Ask, "Which animal displayed more commitment in providing this food: the chicken or the pig?" Allow for responses, and then ask the students why they selected the animal they did.

Continue by stating, "Clearly, the pig had to commit more than the chicken—it cost the pig its life to provide us with ham [or bacon]. Real commitment to Christ is also costly. Total commitment means that we give up ownership of our lives to Him." Read Luke 9:23-24, and then discuss the question Jesus asked in verse 25: "What good is it for a man to gain the whole world, and yet lose or forfeit his very self?"

Ask the students which of their behaviors and actions reflect the Lord's ownership of their lives. Have them name something they would not be willing to do for Jesus. Conclude the discussion by asking the students what they would do if they were in a situation that they knew would result in losing their lives if they admitted that they were Christians.

additional scriptures

1 Chronicles 21:24; Luke 14:25-35; Romans 12:1-2; Philippians 3:7-10

15

fellowship and a bunch of charcoal briquettes

key verse

"If we walk in the light, as he is in the light, we have fellowship with one another, and the blood of Jesus, his Son, purifies us from all sin" (1 John 1:7).

materials needed

a bag of charcoal briquettes
a box of plastic sandwich bags
charcoal grill (if you plan to light the briquettes)

object lesson

To begin the illustration, pour out several charcoal briquettes. (*Note*: This will be messy. Pour the briquettes onto a sheet of newspaper if you are not setting them on fire, or into a charcoal grill. This is actually a great object lesson to use at a picnic, campfire or barbeque, and actually light the briquettes so that students can see the application.)

Say something like, "Fellowship is a lot like this bunch of charcoal briquettes. The thing that makes charcoal work is that when it's lumped together in your barbecue and lit on fire, the briquettes feed off the warmth of the other briquettes. But if you take out one of the briquettes and set it on its own, it will shortly cool off and lose all of its heat. But if you place that lone briquette back in the pile with the other 'on-fire' briquettes, it will once again heat up."

Continue by stating, "We're just like that. We need to be in fellowship with other 'on-fire' Christians to keep our own fire alive. Once we take ourselves out of fellowship with others, we begin to 'cool off' in our relationship with Christ. One of the purposes of fellowship is to be around other on-fire Christians who will challenge you to be all that God desires you to be. Don't miss out. Don't cool off. Hang out with other Christians who will keep your fire alive for Christ."

At the end of the message, give each student a charcoal briquette in a sandwich bag to take home as a reminder of the importance of Christian fellowship.

additional scriptures

Acts 2:42-47; 4:32-35; 1 Corinthians 12:12-26; Galatians 6:2

16

first things first!

key verse

"Seek first his kingdom and his righteousness, and all these things will be given to you as well" (Matthew 6:33).

materials needed

table
large, empty plastic mayonnaise or peanut butter jar with the labels removed
walnuts in the shells
gravel and sand

object lesson

Measure out the exact amount of walnuts, gravel and sand needed to fill the jar to the top. Ideally, everything should fit if you put in the walnuts first, then the gravel, then the sand and finally put the lid on.

Explain that this jar represents a normal day in our lives. Start by placing all the sand in the jar. As you pour, say the sand represents activities such as talking on the phone, texting friends, twittering, watching sports, listening to music, playing video games, and so forth. Next, pour in the gravel and explain that it represents going to school, doing homework, eating, sleeping, spending time with family, and so on.

After you have done this, try to cram as many walnuts as possible into the jar. The walnuts represent an aspect of our daily walk with Christ. One walnut could represent prayer, another Scripture reading, another witnessing, another fellowship with Christians, and so forth. Of course, only a few walnuts will fit, and you will barely be able to put the lid on the jar.

When the jar is nice and full, though still lacking most of the walnuts, pass it around and point out how stressed the jar is—nearly to the point of cracking. Explain that it is important to decide what to put first in our lives. If we start by putting the less important things ahead of spending time with God, not only will we run out of room for Him, but we will be so busy that we stress out and start failing at our other daily activities.

Now empty the jar and reverse the order. First, place all of the walnuts into the jar, explaining the role that each one plays in our lives. Next, pour

in all of the gravel, talking about the importance of going to school, doing homework, spending time with family, eating and sleeping. Finally, pour the sand into the jar, discussing the time we spend for other activities such as hanging out with friends, listening to music, texting, and the like. If you measured correctly and practiced this a time or two, all of the ingredients will fit and the lid can be closed without cracking or stressing the jar.

Conclude the object lesson by reading the key verse in Matthew 6:33. Explain that we often fill our lives with activities and issues that grab our attention. Many of these activities are good and important, but some aren't so good for us, and many are even a waste of our time. It is extremely important that we give our time to the people, activities and issues that are the most important. In everything we do, our lives should reflect that we put God first.

Pick up a few of the walnuts, which represent time spent with God. Explain how if we don't put God first, He will often be crowded out by everything else we do and there will end up being no room for Him in our lives. If we put God first, however, He promises that everything else of importance will fall into place. A godly man named Martin Luther once spoke of the importance of spending time with God among all of the other things we do each day. He said, "I have so much to do that I spend several hours in prayer before I am able to do it."[1] If we want to get everything done in our lives that needs to be done, we must remember to put our relationship with God first. He will take care of the rest.

As a group, discuss what happens when we make our relationship with God our first priority. Have the students give an example of a time when they have put other things first in their lives before God. What was the result? Ask students how their lives would change if they always put God first.

additional scriptures

Psalms 23:1; 37:4; Proverbs 3:6; Galatians 5:25-26; Philippians 4:19

Note

1. Mark Water, compiler, *The New Encyclopedia of Christian Quotations* (Grand Rapids, MI: Baker Books, 2000), p. 764.

17

important functions

key verses

"The eye cannot say to the hand, 'I don't need you!' And the head cannot say to the feet, 'I don't need you!' On the contrary, those parts of the body that seem to be weaker are indispensable" (1 Corinthians 12:21-22).

materials needed

surgical instrument (e.g., scalpel, clamp, suture, surgical tool)

object lesson

Display the surgical instrument and explain what it is and what it does. (*Note*: You can borrow this from a doctor, nurse or surgical-instrument salesperson. This instrument can be small or large, but make sure that it has a significant use, and be sure that you understand what the instrument is used for.) Make the point that although the instrument may be small and ordinary (or some other characteristic), it has an important function. It can't be used for another purpose during surgery because it is designed for a specific function.

Share the key verse in 1 Corinthians 12:21-22, and then explain the importance of each person's contribution to the Body of Christ. Make the point that each person has different skills and gifts that can be used to serve in specific ways. Each person is vitally important in helping the Body of Christ function effectively.

Have each student in the group name two skills or abilities that they have, and then discuss how these skills and abilities can be used to help strengthen, equip and/or encourage the Body of Christ. Ask the group what they would want to do if they could attempt anything for God and were assured that they would not fail.

additional scriptures

Romans 12:3-8; 1 Corinthians 7:7; 11:17-22; 1 Peter 4:10

18

the old made new

key verse

"Therefore, if anyone is in Christ, he is a new creation; the old has gone, the new has come!" (2 Corinthians 5:17).

materials needed

a piece of furniture that has been refinished (a picture of its "before" state would be a good idea) or two pieces of furniture with one in the old state and the other already refinished

object lesson

Read the key verse in 2 Corinthians 5:17, and then hold up the piece of furniture that has been refinished. Explain that this piece of furniture is much like what Paul describes in this passage—an old creation made new. Discuss the following key steps in the process of refinishing furniture to explain how we become new through Christ:

1. The old is stripped away (see Romans 6:1-4,11-14).
2. The furniture is sanded and buffed to make it smooth (see Jeremiah 9:7).
3. The piece is stained or painted to give it the final look (see Galatians 5:16-25).

(*Note*: If you are lucky enough to have a volunteer who refinishes furniture as a job or a hobby, they might be willing to do the work while someone else leads the talk.)

As you (or the other person you have enlisted) go through the process, explain to the group that this is exactly what God does with us as believers. He takes us as we are and rescues us from the trashcan (death). Jesus Christ's death and resurrection is the agent He uses to strip off our old selves (when we realize our sin and come to Christ). Then He sands us clean of our old sin nature (we experience discipline when we go through difficulties). After that, God remakes us into new creations (what He originally intended us to be), just as a furniture refinisher uses stain or paint to restore the original beauty to the piece of furniture.

Give students a few minutes to reflect on how God is dealing with them right now. You might ask them to share where they think they are in God's refinishing process and how having a relationship with Christ has made them a different person. If they have been Christians for a long time, ask how their lives have become more Christlike over the years. Also have them share what sin issue they struggle with the most that they would like God to strip away from their lives.

additional scriptures

Jeremiah 9:7; Zechariah 3:3-4; Romans 6:1-4,11-14; 8:1-9; 12:1-2; 2 Corinthians 5:17; Galatians 5:16-25; Hebrews 12:7-11

19

walking the tightrope

key verse

"What good is it, my brothers, if a man claims to have faith but has no deeds? Can such faith save him?" (James 2:14).

materials needed

a 15-foot length of rope
two stepladders

object lesson

Lay the rope on the floor in a straight line, and then ask for a volunteer who would be willing to help you do this object lesson. (*Note*: Be sure to select someone who won't be crazy enough to try to walk this tightrope when you later suspend it between the two stepladders.) When you have selected the person, instruct him or her to walk the rope—tightrope-style—on the floor.

The volunteer will (hopefully!) do this without any problem. Next, bring out the two stepladders and place one at each end of the rope on the floor. Ask for two strong volunteers to come up to the front, and then instruct them to each pick up one end of the rope and secure the end to the top of their assigned stepladder. This will form an aboveground tightrope. Now ask the original volunteer if he or she is willing to walk across the rope again. When the student declines, have all the volunteers sit down.

Read the key verse in James 2:14. Explain to the group that walking a tightrope placed on the floor is easy because there's no risk. However, walking a tightrope that has been lifted off the ground is an entirely different matter. When the risk factor is added, most people won't attempt to do it.

Continue by stating that having faith in Jesus is a lot like walking on that tightrope. Many people find it easy to believe in Jesus when there is no risk involved—when nothing is asked or expected of them. But real

faith requires action, not just belief. Real faith is displayed even when believing in Jesus gets hard. It is demonstrated when our friends reject us because we believe in Jesus, and we choose to keep believing in Him anyway. It is demonstrated when we turn the other cheek when we are put down, hurt or persecuted by others. It is demonstrated when we show love to someone who is unpopular or disliked even if this results in us being ridiculed by others for associating with that person. Belief plus action equals real faith!

Next, share the following story of a man named Blondin, a famous tightrope walker in the 1800s, who once strung a tightrope across Niagara Falls.

> Before ten thousand screaming people [Blondin] inched his way from the Canadian side of the falls to the United States side. When he got there, the crowd began shouting his name: "Blondin! Blondin! Blondin! Blondin!"
>
> Finally he raised his arms, quieted the crowd and shouted to them, "I am Blondin! Do you believe in me?"
>
> The crowd shouted back, "We believe! We believe! We believe!"
>
> Again he quieted the crowd, and once more he shouted to them, "I'm going back across the tightrope, but this time I'm going to carry someone on my back. Do you believe I can do that?"
>
> The crowd yelled, "We believe! We believe!"
>
> He quieted them one more time and then he asked, "Who will be that person?" The crowd went silent. Nothing.
>
> Finally, out of the crowd stepped one man. He climbed on Blondin's shoulders, and for the next three-and-a-half hours, Blondin inched his way back across the tightrope to the Canadian side of the falls.[1]

Conclude by explaining that the point of this story is that while 10,000 people stood there that day chanting, "We believe! We believe!" only one person really believed enough to volunteer to be carried across on Blondin's back. Believing is not just saying that we accept the fact. Believing involves putting our lives in the hands of the One in whom we say we believe. This is not usually the easy or comfortable way to go. It involves risk on our part and a belief that we serve an all-knowing and all-powerful God who will take care of us.

As a group, discuss when it is the hardest to believe in God and when it is the easiest. Have the students give an example of a time when they have taken a risk that demonstrated their faith in Jesus. Ask them what difficult situation they are currently facing that will require them to step out and show their faith in God's trustworthiness.

additional scriptures

Matthew 5:16; 2 Thessalonians 1:4,11; 1 Timothy 6:11-12; Titus 3:8; James 1:22

Note

1. Tony Campolo, *You Can Make a Difference* (Waco, TX: Word, 1984), p. 14.

20

will it stand?

key verse

"Everyone who hears these words of mine and puts them into practice is like a wise man who built his house on the rock" (Matthew 7:24).

materials needed

three (or more) pieces of poster board
three (or more) paper grocery bags
one (or more) deck of playing cards
Legos or Tinkertoys
miscellaneous items that could be put together to form a structure

preparation

Ahead of time, fill each paper bag with one of the following items:

Bag 1: the deck of playing cards
Bag 2: a miscellaneous collection of items that really do not match
Bag 3: Legos or Tinkertoys

If you have a large group, you may need to prepare more bags with the same mix of items so that when you form teams there aren't more than 10 to 12 in a group.

object lesson

Have students form three teams. Have each team sit around a piece of poster board. Instruct the teams to use the contents of their bags to build a house on the poster board.

Give a time limit of 5 to 10 minutes. When the time is up, walk around to the different groups and talk about each of the houses they built. Discuss the sturdiness of the house, the structure of the house, the students' creativity and, most importantly, the ability of the various houses to stand up under pressure.

Have a volunteer read the parable of the wise and foolish builders in Matthew 7:24-27. As a group, discuss which of the houses the students built is more like the house on the sand and which is more like the house built on the good foundation. Discuss what made the difference between the two houses, and then ask students what makes the difference in our lives. Discuss how we hear God's words and put them into practice, and ask each student to assess which of the houses best represents their lives and foundation.

additional scriptures

Psalm 37:23-26; 1 Corinthians 3:10-17; Ephesians 2:19-22; 1 Peter 2:4-6

21

the windows of our soul

key verse

"Do not conform any longer to the pattern of this world, but be transformed by the renewing of your mind. Then you will be able to test and approve what God's will is—his good, pleasing and perfect will" (Romans 12:2).

materials needed

an old window frame with four panes of glass (available from remodeling sites, architectural recyclers or through carpenters or glaziers)
a piece of clear Plexiglas (available at most hardware stores)
a folding chair
a foot-long piece of metal pipe
a canvas drop cloth or an old blanket

preparation

Replace one glass pane with the Plexiglas and, if needed, use dirt to make the new pane look like the old ones. Lay the drop cloth on the floor and prop the frame on the folding chair set on the drop cloth.

object lesson

Begin by asking the group, "What changes need to be made when we give our lives to Christ?" After several responses, ask why we often resist the influence that Jesus wants to have in our lives. Allow for responses, and then share a personal example of an area in which you struggled, such as rebellion against your parents or disobeying a school rule. (*Note*: Don't be too revealing here. Leaders often make themselves out to be folk heroes when they talk about their life of sin. Students might think, *My youth leader did this and it worked out okay, so I can try it too!* Be sure to relate the consequences of your wrong actions.)

As you describe the time when you failed because you relied on your old ways, pick up the metal pipe and casually smash out a pane of glass from the window frame. (*Caution*: You need only to tap the glass; the pipe

will easily break it. The point is made through the glass breaking, not through seeing how far the glass will fly.)

Continue sharing, and as you talk about wanting to do things your own way instead of God's way, use the pipe to break the second and then the third pane of glass. Ask the group how Christ helps us to clean up the messes we've made.

Transition by sharing about how your growing faith enabled you to trust Jesus with your life, and that it was because of this trust that He began to change you. Tap the Plexiglas pane (you can hit it harder than you did the glass) and point out that when we are walking with Jesus, He will provide the strength to do God's will for our lives.

additional scriptures

Proverbs 3:3,5-6; Philippians 1:27-28; 2:5; 4:13; 1 John 2:3-6

22

a messy situation

key verses

"For all have sinned and fall short of the glory of God, and are justified freely by his grace through the redemption that came by Christ Jesus" (Romans 3:23-24).

materials needed

a chalkboard or wall covered with a white sheet or white paper, or a whiteboard

a clear sheet of plastic large enough to cover the board and the floor directly in front of it (a paint drop cloth is perfect!)

masking tape

various foods (ketchup, mustard, cooked spinach, honey, egg, jam, syrup, anything colorful and messy)

liquid dishwashing soap in a plastic bottle

a rag or sponge

a pair of rubber gloves

object lesson

Begin by talking about how in the beginning we were created perfect and sinless (use the chalkboard or whiteboard to represent our condition before the Fall). Tape the plastic drop cloth over the board. As you talk about the Fall of man, start throwing the food items one at a time at the plastic-covered board.

As you throw each food at specific spots on the plastic (try to keep the different spots separate at first), talk about the different sins that tempt your students. After you have covered the board with the food, put on the rubber gloves.

Squirt some dishwashing liquid on the board and attempt to wipe it off. As you do this, explain how we humans often try to attain salvation by our own works. Make sure to make a bigger mess than was previously there. Then explain how our attempts to attain salvation on our own make our lives messier and messier. Smear everything around to make it even worse.

Now tell the students that God took the initiative to help us in our situation by sending Jesus Christ to remove our sin nature, and that if we receive the gift of Christ dying for us, we will be made clean again. Peel off the plastic to reveal the clean board.

additional scriptures

Psalm 51:1-12; Isaiah 1:18; John 3:16-18; Romans 5:6-8; 6:23; 10:9-10

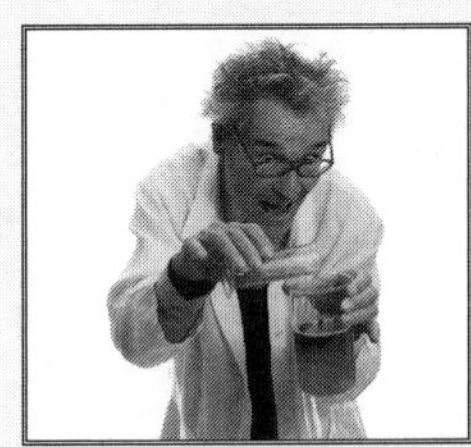

23

never lost

key verses

"God has given us eternal life, and this life is in his Son. He who has the Son has life; he who does not have the Son of God does not have life" (1 John 5:11-12).

preparation

a handheld Global Positioning System (GPS) unit (you shouldn't have too much trouble finding or renting one)

object lesson

Invite students to share a recent experience in which they got lost. (You might explain a personal experience of your own to get them started.) Discuss the frustration of being lost, and then show the GPS unit. State that the GPS unit works by receiving signals from satellites orbiting the earth and that this unit can keep track of where you are anywhere in the world. With a GPS, you can always know where you are going, and you should never get lost.

Now explain that the Bible—God's Word—is our spiritual GPS unit. God has assured us in His Word that we can have eternal life, and when we read and study the Bible, we will learn how to navigate through this life. With the Bible as our guide, we will never be lost!

Ask students if they have ever doubted that they are really Christians. If so, what caused them to doubt? Read the key verses in 1 John 5:11-13 and discuss how a person can know whether or not he or she has eternal life. Discuss how the Bible serves as a guide for life. Ask how students think their lives would be different if they consulted the Bible more often.

additional scriptures

John 14:18-19; 2 Timothy 3:16-17; 6:12; Hebrews 4:12-13; 2 Peter 1:10-11

salvation & redemption

24

only one key turns the lock

key verses

"Then know this, you and all the people of Israel: It is by the name of Jesus Christ of Nazareth, whom you crucified but whom God raised from the dead, that this man stands before you healed. He is 'the stone you builders rejected, which has become the capstone.' Salvation is found in no one else, for there is no other name under heaven given to men by which we must be saved" (Acts 4:10-12).

materials needed

a padlock
the key that works in the padlock
other keys that don't work (try to find some keys that look similar to the key that opens the padlock)

object lesson

Show the padlock and a key that doesn't work, and then ask students if they believe the key will open the lock. After they respond, demonstrate how the key doesn't work to turn the lock. Explain that no matter how sincere they might be or how deeply they believe this particular key will open the lock, it still won't open the lock. Try the other keys that won't work. Finally, select the key that opens the lock and open it.

Read the key verses in Acts 4:10-12, and then explain that no matter how deeply someone may believe that a certain key will open a lock, it must be the correct key in order for it to work. Some keys might look as if they would open the lock, but they still don't work. In the same way, no matter how sincere a person might be or how sure he or she is that their good works will get them into heaven, a faith in a "wrong key" will not open the correct door. A saving faith is more than just believing that God exists. True faith must be placed in the right *Person*, and the Bible teaches that saving faith is based on belief in Jesus Christ alone.

Have students discuss what they would say to someone who believes there are many ways to God and that Christianity is just one of those ways. Ask them how they would respond to someone who rejects Christianity because it seems too exclusive to require people to believe in Jesus in order to get into heaven.

additional scriptures

Proverbs 14:12; John 3:16-18; 14:6; Acts 16:31; 1 John 5:11-12

25

melting away

key verse

"Let us not become weary in doing good, for at the proper time we will reap a harvest if we do not give up" (Galatians 6:9).

materials needed

an ice cream cone (or bar) for each student and leader

object lesson

Declare it an ice cream cone event and hand out ice cream cones to everyone, reserving one for yourself. (*Note*: This would be a great hot-weather activity.) Have everyone sit down, and then begin to talk about what it means to serve Jesus.

As they eat and you talk, let the cone melt over your hand and onto the floor. Make no effort to stop it, clean it up or keep the drips off the floor. (If you have carpet on the floor, you might want to stand with your hand over a table or a chair unless you really want the church custodian on your case!) Students will bring attention to your plight, but ignore them. Simply continue on and let the cone melt. (*Note*: To hasten the effect, you can sit with a fan blowing on your hand—moving air will help the ice cream melt faster, especially if it is in hot weather.)

After your ice cream cone has melted, explain to the group that just as you shouldn't have allowed your ice cream cone to melt, the students shouldn't allow their lives and opportunities to melt away. The choice is theirs: Will they take the opportunities that God offers them in life, or will they simply let them melt away and miss the wonderful things God has to offer?

Note that everyone in the group took the opportunity to enjoy the ice cream except you. Point out that they (hopefully) tried to tell you to eat the ice cream before it melted, but you just let it melt. Relate their comments to how others—parents, teachers, friends, youth leaders—try to encourage them when they are missing an opportunity, and that they need to listen to the wisdom of others.

Conclude by discussing with the group the ways that people often waste their lives. Ask them how they can use their time wisely, and have them evaluate what the most important activities are in their schedules and which ones might be wasting too much of their valuable time. Discuss how they can know God's will for their lives.

additional scriptures

Psalm 31:14-15; Ecclesiastes 3:1-8; 8:5; Matthew 25:14-30; Ephesians 5:15-17

26

the road signs of life

key verse

"A simple man believes anything, but a prudent man gives thought to his steps" (Proverbs 14:15).

materials needed

construction paper or poster board
color markers

preparation

Before your meeting, construct the following road signs, either on pieces of construction paper or on poster board. If possible, get students to help you. Add some creative artwork to make the signs look authentic.

- Under Construction
- Enter at Your Own Risk
- Detour
- Rough Road Ahead
- Winding Road Ahead
- Speed Limit
- Dangerous Curve
- Yield
- Slippery When Wet
- Stop
- Caution
- Any other signs you can think of

(*Note*: You can also purchase replicas of these road signs at a learning supply store.)

object lesson

Post the road signs around the meeting room. As you begin the message, ask the students to stand under the sign that best represents their lives or relationships with God right now. Don't give any definitions for the signs; just let them select their own meanings for how the signs apply to their lives or relationships with God. Ask several volunteers to explain their choices. This is a great way to get to know students and how they view themselves and their relationship with God.

additional scriptures

Psalm 138:8; Proverbs 3:5-6; Matthew 7:13; Philippians 1:6

27

the value remains

key verse

"How great is the love the Father has lavished on us, that we should be called children of God! And that is what we are!" (1 John 3:1).

materials needed

a $20 bill
wet dirt (just shy of being mud) in a small container

object lesson

Hold the $20 bill up and ask the students how much they think the bill is worth. Next, perform the following series of actions on the bill, and after each action ask the students how much they think the bill is worth:

1. Crinkle the bill up just a bit.
2. Wad the bill up tightly in your hand, and then smooth it out.
3. Rub it in the wet dirt.
4. Rip the bill slightly.

After the last action, make the point that no matter how crumpled or dirty or torn the bill is, it is still worth $20.

Read the key verse in 1 John 3:1 and explain that many people believe that they are not worth anything, especially to God. Some believe this because of the sins that they have committed, while others believe this about themselves because of the sins that have been committed against them. However, it is important to realize that God loves and values each of us, no matter what we have done or what has been done to us. God values us for who we are.

Ask the students how their behavior affects what they believe God thinks and feels about them. Discuss how someone else's behavior toward them can also have an effect on how they believe God thinks and feels about them. Finally, ask students what they think God would say if He were to tell someone about them. Explain the difference that God's love should make in their lives in terms of how they feel about themselves.

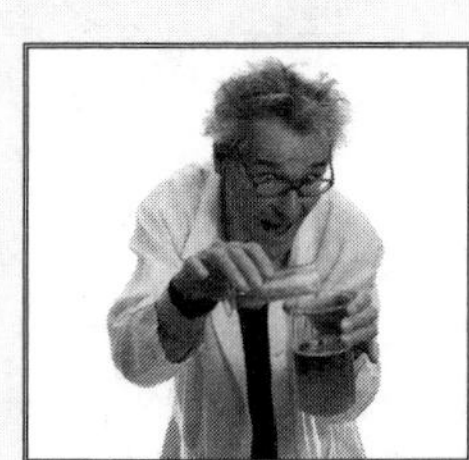

additional scriptures

Psalm 139:1-16; Jeremiah 31:3; John 8:1-11; Romans 5:6-8; 8:35-39; Ephesians 2:1-10

28

who we really are

key verse

"Circumcise your hearts, therefore, and do not be stiff-necked any longer" (Deuteronomy 10:16).

materials needed

a clear drinking glass, half filled with water

object lesson

Begin by pointing out that many Christians act one way when they're at church or church-related activities and another way when they're at school or with friends who don't go to church. Facilitate a brief discussion using the following questions:

- Has there been a time when you acted differently around your non-Christian friends than you would have acted around your Christian friends?
- What caused you to act differently in those situations?
- In what situations are you most tempted to act differently?

Allow for a few responses, and then have students silently consider the following question: "When someone's behavior changes depending on the people around him or her, which of his or her behaviors reflect the real person inside?"

Hold up the glass and pour some water out onto the floor. Ask the group, "Why did water spill on the floor?" Allow for a few responses, and then point out that the main reason the water spilled from the glass was because there was water in the glass to begin with. Use this illustration to make the following connection: "The words we say and the actions we take reflect who we really are inside."

Explain that our words and actions reveal the condition of our hearts. Challenge students to look up the additional Scriptures listed below and to take time to examine their lives. Explain that God knows that none of us are perfect, but He wants us to admit to ourselves where we are in our lives. He does not want us to be phony or try to hide from Him. Confessing our faults and sins to God is the most important step for cleaning out the junk in our lives. When we confess our sins, we can know for sure that God will forgive us and restore us to a right relationship with Him.

additional scriptures

Jeremiah 17:9; Matthew 15:18-19; Luke 6:43-45; 1 John 1:8-9

29

filling our minds

key verse

"Finally, brothers, whatever is true, whatever is noble, whatever is right, whatever is pure, whatever is lovely, whatever is admirable—if anything is excellent or praiseworthy—think about such things" (Philippians 4:8).

materials needed

blender
extension cord (if needed)
vanilla ice cream
milk
chocolate syrup
small plastic or paper cups
ketchup
soy sauce
Tabasco sauce
a large spoon
sardines or a fish from the grocery store
spinach
clam juice
any other unpalatable items you can think of

object lesson

Set up the blender on a flat surface. Begin by talking about the things that we put into our minds and how they affect us. This is an illustration in two parts. For the first part, make a chocolate milkshake using the vanilla ice cream, milk and chocolate syrup. After making the milkshake, pour the shake into a few cups and give them to a few students in the group. Talk about the ingredients you've put into the blender to make the milkshake. The delicious ingredients you put into the blender affected what came out of the blender.

For the second part of the illustration, make another milk shake with the vanilla ice cream, milk, chocolate syrup, and then begin to add the rest of the listed items. As you add the other items, talk about the garbage we sometimes put into our minds—pornography, vulgar music, terrible movies, and the like. As you finish with your concoction, ask if anyone would now like to have a milkshake.

Conclude by explaining to the group that what they put into their minds truly does affect what comes out—and it affects how others view them. Discuss Philippians 4:8 and the things with which we need to be filling our minds: those things that are true, noble, right, pure, lovely, admirable, excellent and praiseworthy.

additional scriptures

Proverbs 4:23-27; Romans 12:1-2; Hebrews 4:12; James 1:14-15,21

30

fish in a blender

key verse

"Flee from sexual immorality. All other sins a man commits are outside his body, but he who sins sexually sins against his own body" (1 Corinthians 6:18).

materials needed

blender
small table
glass of water
extension cord
sharp knife
fish (from the grocery store)

preparation

Before the meeting begins, place the blender on the small table along with the other items. Use the extension cord to plug in your blender to the nearest electrical outlet.

object lesson

Before you begin this object lesson, explain that God designed sex to be reserved for the marriage relationship only. In this lesson, you will be comparing sex within marriage to using equipment properly. If you don't use an appliance for what it is designed, the results could be disastrous!

Hold up the fish. Ask your students, "If you wanted to fillet this fish, what object would you use?" (*Note*: Your students may not know what "fillet" means. Either provide a sample from the grocery store, or tell them that it means "to cut a thin boneless sideways slice from the fish.") Tell your group that you will first try the blender to see if that is the proper equipment for filleting the fish. Pour the glass of water into the blender, and then drop your fish in.

Continue to talk about the danger of using improper equipment. Set your blender on puree and let 'er rip! Your point will be made for you. Af-

ter this, hold up the knife and tell your group that this is the proper instrument for filleting a fish.

Conclude the illustration by explaining how getting involved sexually before marriage is like trying to fillet a fish with a blender. The resulting consequences are a mess. It's not what you want or what God had in mind for the gift of sex.

additional scriptures

Genesis 1:26-28; 2:20-25; Matthew 19:4-6; 1 Corinthians 6:19-20; 1 Thessalonians 4:3-7

31

dealing with past sins

key verse

"Come now, let us reason together," says the Lord. "Though your sins are like scarlet, they shall be as white as snow; though they are red as crimson, they shall be like wool" (Isaiah 1:18).

materials needed

clear drinking glass
water
blue food coloring
liquid bleach

preparation

Fill the glass about two-thirds full with water.

object lesson

Begin by explaining how sin darkens our lives. As you talk, list specific sins and place a drop of blue food coloring in the glass of water for each sin you list. (Be careful not to use too many drops of food coloring.)

Next, discuss how Jesus died and was resurrected to cleanse us and remove all of our sins, guilt and shame. As you speak about what Jesus has done for us, pour some liquid bleach (take care not to splash it onto your clothing or carpet) into the tinted water. The bleach will dissolve the food color and return the water to clear—though some yellowish tint may remain. (*Note*: While red food coloring would work better symbolically, blue food coloring dissolves better than red in this object lesson.)

Share the key verse in Isaiah 1:18 with the group, and then explain how the sins of our past can make it difficult for us to experience the freedom that God desires for us to have in the present and in the future. The blood of Christ that cleanses us from all sin is like the bleach in the colored water. When we come to God and humbly confess our sins and ask Him to

forgive us and give us a clean slate, He grants our request! Our sinful past is immediately cleansed and wiped away forever.

Conclude the lesson by discussing with the group how it makes them feel to know that God is willing and able to forgive any and all of their past sins. What difference should it make in how they live their lives, knowing that God forgives their sins? What did it cost God to provide salvation and redeem them from their sins? Also talk about why so many people refuse to come to God to confess their sins and ask for His forgiveness. Ask students how their lives reflect their gratitude to God for His forgiveness.

additional scriptures

Psalm 51; John 10:10; Galatians 5:1; Hebrews 9:14; 10:19-22; 1 John 1:9

32

flushed away

key verse

"For the wages of sin is death, but the gift of God is eternal life in Christ Jesus our Lord" (Romans 6:23).

materials needed

an old toilet (used toilets can be found at remodeling projects, building-supply recycling places or even a junkyard—the dirtier and more beat up the better)
concrete blocks or bricks
lots of water (both dirty water and clean)
child-sized plastic swimming pool
whiteboard, chalkboard or flip chart and pens or chalk
small slips of paper and pens or pencils (optional)

object lesson

Set up the toilet securely on the concrete blocks or bricks in the plastic swimming pool. Fill the toilet bowl with scummy water—either add dirt or garbage to the water or make the church custodian ecstatic and offer to wash the floor at the church. Then, after letting the water sit for a day or two—the smellier the better—pour the gray water into the bowl. Fill the tank with clean water. (*Note*: This lesson is best done outside, but just remember that if you choose to do it inside, you will eventually need to get the water out of the meeting room!)

As you discuss sin, have the students list the sins they see being committed around them every day. You might want to bring in examples found in news articles, song lyrics and/or movie and TV themes to get the sharing started. Write down the group's responses on the board or flipchart. Guide students to respond with specific examples of everyday sins. (As an option, you could also have the students write out the sins with which they struggle on a small slip of paper. Have them fold the paper and hold on to it until you give them further instructions.)

Liken sin to the dirty water in the toilet bowl. Explain that it's smelly and contaminated and that there's nothing we can do on our own to clean

the water. We can try to hide the smell by using air fresheners to cover up the odor, but this will only mask the problem—not get rid of it—and will only last a short time. We can pour disinfectant into the tank, but that won't get rid of the dirt, and the contamination will return.

Now explain that this is just how it is with our own sin. There is nothing we can do on our own to rid our lives of sin—we need help in cleaning up the mess. As we confess our sin to God, He cleanses us. He flushes out all the filth in our lives, and we are clean. (*Note*: If you elected to have the students write down some of their sins on a slip of paper, have them throw the papers into the toilet at this time. Use this as a visual image to personalize their confession and cleansing in God's eyes.) Now flush the toilet. The dirty water will be flushed out, and the bowl will be filled with clean water.

As a group, discuss the ways sin can harm us. Ask the students how the sins they commit directly affect other people. Ask them what the difference is between being sorry for their sin and exhibiting true repentance. Also ask whether they think confession means they can sin and still be pals with God. Does God hope for something else from their confession?

additional scriptures

Romans 3:23-24; 12:1-2; Galatians 5:16-21; Ephesians 4:22-31; 5:3-8; Hebrews 3:13; 1 John 1:6-9; 2:1-6,15-17

33

nailing sin to the cross

key verse

"He was pierced for our transgressions, he was crushed for our iniquities; the punishment that brought us peace was upon him, and by his wounds we are healed" (Isaiah 53:5).

materials needed

a cross made of 2 x 4s (size of the cross will depend on your group's size)
3 x 5-inch index cards (enough for one for each group member)
pens or pencils
a box of nails
hammers (several if possible)
worship music

object lesson

During the message or Bible study, have the cross available for you to refer to while you are speaking. Use the cross as the central visual point of the message or study time.

At the end of the time together, give each student a 3 x 5-inch index card and a pencil or pen. On the cards, have them write down either an area of their lives that they need to surrender to Christ or an area of sin with which they are struggling. Tell them not to sign their names—this will be in the strictest confidence. Supply nails and hammers and have them come up to the cross and physically nail their cards to the cross.

Play some worship music during this time to create a worshipful atmosphere. The sound of worship music, singing and the nailing on the cross are unforgettable.

additional scriptures

Matthew 27:33-54; Mark 8:34-38; 15:22-39; Luke 23:33-47; John 19:17-30; Hebrews 7:26-28; 9:13-14,28; 1 Peter 2:22-25

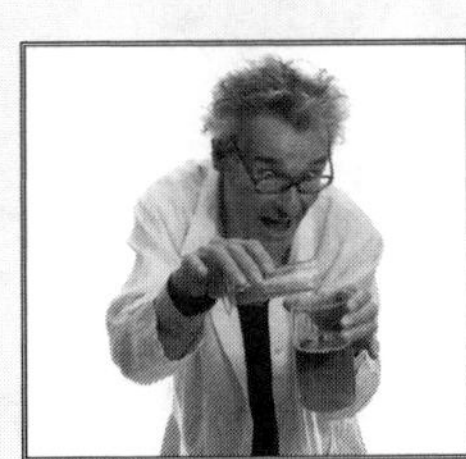

34

the poisoned piñata

key verse

"If we claim to have fellowship with him yet walk in the darkness, we lie and do not live by the truth" (1 John 1:6).

materials needed

a piñata
garbage (coffee grounds, egg shells, fruit rinds)
a stick or bat
a blindfold
a plastic drop cloth
another piñata filled with candy (optional)

preparation

This object lesson works well as part of a big event with your youth group. Advertise the meeting for a few weeks before the event, highlighting the piñata theme and the great fun and treats to be had. Before the meeting, fill the piñata with the garbage and set it up over the drop cloth (or set this up outside). (You can also prepare a second piñata filled with candy or bring candy to give to the students after the lesson.)

object lesson

As the meeting begins, act excited and let students believe that there is some great stuff inside the piñata. Blindfold the first batter and let him or her have a few swings at the piñata. As more batters take their turns and the piñata breaks, students will dive for the treats before they realize that the piñata's bounty is really garbage.

Ask the group, "Were you surprised by what came out of the piñata?" Explain that people can be similar to this piñata—they can work hard and look like committed Christians on the outside, but on the inside they really aren't committed to Jesus at all. Ask a few volunteers to share about

some of the times they've gone through the motions of *looking* like a good Christian when their hearts weren't where they should have been.

additional scriptures

Matthew 7:15-23; 23:27-28; Titus 1:16; 1 John 1:8; 2:4

35

sucked in by pride

key verse

"The pride of your heart has deceived you, you who live in the clefts of the rocks and make your home on the heights, you who say to yourself, 'Who can bring me down to the ground?' " (Obadiah 1:3).

materials needed

one hard-boiled egg (peeled)
a glass milk bottle
two matches

preparation

Before the lesson, boil an egg and peel it. Make sure that it is large enough to sit on top of the empty milk bottle without falling into it.

object lesson

Place the egg on top of the bottle. Confidently state the obvious: "This egg doesn't look like it can fall into the bottle, right?" Pick up the egg, and then light both matches and drop them into the milk bottle. Immediately replace the egg on top of the milk bottle. The matches will burn up the oxygen in the milk bottle, creating a vacuum that will then suck the egg into the bottle.

As you are waiting for the egg to fall into the bottle, explain that at times each of us can fall into the trap of believing that we are so spiritually strong that we are invulnerable to Satan's traps. When this occurs, pride creeps in, and we may think that we are impervious to getting involved in certain behaviors—especially addictive behaviors such as sexual promiscuity, drugs, alcohol, gambling, and the like. Explain that this is a dangerous thing to believe—spiritual pride is a trap that Satan sets for us. Just when we think we can't fall, we become most susceptible to falling. We have to always be on guard against pride!

Ask the group if they believe it is possible to get to the place in our lives where we don't have to worry about falling to some temptation. Why or why not? Read Proverbs 16:18 and ask the group what this verse means. Discuss ways that the students can help one another avoid spiritual pride.

additional scriptures

Psalm 18:27; Proverbs 16:18; 29:23; Matthew 23:12; Luke 14:11; Galatians 6:1; James 3:13; 4:6-10; 1 Peter 5:5-9

36

tough to break

key verse

"Don't you know that when you offer yourselves to someone to obey him as slaves, you are slaves to the one whom you obey—whether you are slaves to sin, which leads to death, or to obedience, which leads to righteousness?" (Romans 6:16).

materials needed

a spool of thread
scissors

object lesson

Choose a student volunteer (this works best if you select an athletic type). Wrap a single thread once around the student, across his or her arms, and then tie the thread. Instruct the volunteer to break free, which will be easy for him or her to do.

Next, wrap the thread three times around the student and tie it. Ask the volunteer to break free. It will be more difficult to break free, but he or she should be able to do it. Repeat this exercise, wrapping more and more thread around the student each time until he or she is no longer able to break free. When the volunteer cannot escape, use the scissors to cut him or her free.

Share the key verse in Romans 6:16, and then explain that habits—whether good or bad—are formed by repetition. In the beginning, habits are easy to break, but with repetition and time, these habits become more and more difficult to escape. If they form bad habits, these will be harmful to them and difficult to break. However, if they form good habits—such as daily Scripture reading and prayer—these will be beneficial to their lives and will help them to grow in Christ. Be sure to make the point that God can set us free from bad habits in the same way that you cut the student free with the scissors.

Conclude the lesson by asking the group if they think anyone intentionally sets out to develop bad habits. Discuss why people often form these bad habits, even when they know they are harmful. You might also

ask them to list some of the common sinful habits that people develop, discussing which of them are easy to break and which ones are more difficult. Finally, ask students what advice they would give to someone who wanted to break a bad habit.

additional scriptures

Romans 6:18; 7:15-20; 1 Corinthians 6:12; Galatians 5:1; Philippians 4:13; Hebrews 12:1-2; James 1:13-15; 2 Peter 2:19; 1 John 1:6-10

37

a box of potential

key verses

"Search me, O God, and know my heart; test me and know my anxious thoughts. See if there is any offensive way in me, and lead me in the way everlasting" (Psalm 139:23-24).

materials needed

two identical boxes
paper
a $5 bill

preparation

Fill one box with paper and the other with paper and an envelope containing the $5 bill. Be sure to wrap both boxes identically.

object lesson

Display the boxes on a table at the front of the room. Ask for two volunteers to come up to the front of the room. Have one of the volunteers pick one of the boxes to open, and then give the other box to the other person. Tell them not to open the boxes yet. Then tell the group that inside one of the boxes is a $5 bill, while the other box contains nothing. Ask the group and the volunteers to guess which box contains the five dollars.

After a minute or two of discussion, have the volunteers open their boxes. The one who finds the $5 bill may keep it. Have the volunteers sit down, but leave the boxes and wrappings on the table. Refer to the wrappings as you ask the following questions and introduce your message:

1. Did you believe the box that you selected had the $5 bill in it? Why or why not?
2. What was the only way to find out which box contained the $5 bill?

Conclude the illustration by talking about how God judges potential and value by what is *inside* a person rather than what is on the *outside*. The

outside may look the same, but it's what's inside that matters. Stress that the empty box is like a lot of students today who try to look good on the outside but are empty on the inside.

additional scriptures

1 Samuel 16:7-13; Psalm 139:1-18; Matthew 10:29-31; Ephesians 2:8-10

38

faith and works

key verses

"Faith by itself, if it is not accompanied by action, is dead. But someone will say, 'You have faith; I have deeds.' Show me your faith without deeds, and I will show you my faith by what I do" (James 2:17-18).

materials needed

a scooter

object lesson

Display the scooter, and then ask for a volunteer to demonstrate how the scooter works (or demonstrate it yourself). Discuss what it takes to ride a scooter successfully. Make the point that it takes two important things to be able to ride a scooter: (1) balance; and (2) the ability to use one foot to propel the scooter. Without balance, you would fall off; and without using your foot to propel yourself, you wouldn't go anywhere even if you maintained your balance.

Read the key verses in James 2:17-18 and explain that riding a scooter can be compared to being a growing Christian. In order to make the Christian life work, you need two important things: faith and works. Without faith, your works may be helpful to other people, but they won't make you a Christian. Without works, your faith will be sterile and you won't grow in Christ or be a witness to others. Faith and works together will cause your Christian life to grow in leaps and bounds. You'll go places for God! (You could ride off on the scooter to demonstrate this point.)

Conclude the lesson by discussing with the group what James's statement "faith by itself . . . is dead" means. Ask students what makes works without faith just as dead as faith without works. Have them describe a time when they tried to do works in their own power—without relying on faith.

additional scriptures

Galatians 5:6; 1 Thessalonians 1:3; James 2:24; 1 Peter 2:12; Revelation 2:19

39

the importance of roots

key verse

"Since he has no root, he lasts only a short time. When trouble or persecution comes because of the word, he quickly falls away" (Matthew 13:21).

materials needed

two identical, healthy, potted flowering plants

preparation

About a week before the lesson, remove one plant from the pot. Cut off all of the root system, leaving only the foliage and flowers, and then repot the plant. Allow time for the foliage and flowers to wither.

object lesson

Display the potted plants. Explain that you bought these identical plants on the same day, but that now one is healthy while the other is dead. Show students that both are in the same kind of pots, both have been given the same amount of water, and both have been placed side by side and have received equal amounts of heat and light.

Ask the group what they think the problem is, and then pull the dead plant out of the soil, revealing its dead root system. After this, pull the healthy plant out of its pot, revealing its healthy root system. Then share the parable of the sower in Matthew 13:1-23, emphasizing the key verse in Matthew 13:21. Explain that just as a healthy root system is necessary for a plant's survival, so too a healthy root system is necessary for our spiritual survival.

Ask the group what they think they need to do to develop their own healthy, spiritual root systems. Then have the students rate the status of their own spiritual growth on a scale of 1 to 5 (1 being unhealthy and 5 being healthy), and ask them to explain the reasons for rating themselves as they did. Finally, have the students evaluate the issue or issues in their lives that currently presents the biggest threat to their spiritual growth.

Come up with some steps they can take this week to strengthen their spiritual root system.

additional scriptures

John 15:1-8; Romans 12:1; Ephesians 3:16-19; 5:15-20; 6:18; Colossians 2:6-7; 2 Timothy 3:16-17; Hebrews 10:24-25; James 5:16

40

ready to explode

key verses

"'In your anger do not sin': Do not let the sun go down while you are still angry, and do not give the devil a foothold" (Ephesians 4:26-27).

materials needed

two medium-sized glass jars
large baking pan with sides
baking soda
white vinegar
water

object lesson

Begin the object lesson by holding up one of the jars. State that all of us are like this empty container, and that as we go through our day we constantly encounter situations that will cause us tension. As you explain this, set the jar in the large baking pan and pour in some of the baking soda. Continue to add the baking powder to the jar, listing the various tensions that might come up in a student's day (such as homework pressures, disappointments, issues with family, and the like).

Now explain that at some point during our day, we may encounter a situation that will make us angry. State that it is at these times that we need to rely on the strength of the Lord to help us diffuse the situation so that we don't explode at other people or do things in our anger that will cause us to sin. Pour some of the water into the glass jar. Explain that this jar represents those people who turn to the Lord in prayer when they encounter a situation that makes them angry. These individuals are able to diffuse their anger without letting it get the best of them and causing them to sin.

Remove the first jar and set the second empty jar on the baking sheet in its place. Now state that you are going to look at a person who allows the problems in his or her life to build up and does not turn to the Lord when conflict arises. Add the baking powder to the jar, but this time pour in the white vinegar. The mixture of the baking powder and the white

vinegar will cause the mixture to bubble up and "explode" over the top of the jar.

Conclude the object lesson by reading the key verses in Ephesians 4:26-27. Explain that while each of us will get angry at times, we need to make sure that we do not let that anger get out of control and cause us to sin. We do this by taking those situations to God and relying on His strength. We submit to His will in the situation and ask Him to guide our actions and responses.

Proverbs 14:17; 19:11; 25:28; Matthew 5:23-24; Romans 12:2; James 1:19; 4:7

41

a shaky foundation

key verse

"The rain came down, the streams rose, and the winds blew and beat against that house; yet it did not fall, because it had its foundation on the rock" (Matthew 7:25).

materials needed

Jenga® game

preparation

Before the meeting, borrow or purchase a Jenga® game and use it to set up a block tower on a flat surface.

object lesson

Begin by asking your group, "What are some of the shaky foundations people might build their lives on?" Allow the group to respond. After each reply, pull out one block from the stack and replace it on the top of the stack. You can even have students in your group remove a block as they reply to the question.

Add a few responses of your own as you continue to pull out blocks from the stack. Eventually, the stack will fall over because of the faulty foundation. Continue the message or study by discussing why manmade foundations are so shaky. What makes a life foundation either strong or weak? What needs to happen to a building on an unstable foundation? How can an unstable building be corrected? Why do we need to build a firm foundation on Jesus Christ? What tools and equipment do we need to build such a strong foundation?

additional scriptures

Joshua 1:7-9; Psalm 127:1; Luke 6:46-49; John 14:21; 1 Corinthians 3:10-17; Ephesians 2:19-22; 1 Peter 2:4-8

42

staying strong

key verse

"Surely I am with you always, to the very end of the age" (Matthew 28:20).

materials needed

two large balloons
transparent tape
sewing needle

preparation

Before the meeting, inflate and tie off the balloons. Place a 2-inch strip of tape at one end of one of the balloons. Smooth over the tape to remove the air bubbles and make it as transparent as possible.

object lesson

Pick up the sewing needle and the balloon without the tape and hold them up to the group. Begin the lesson by explaining that when we try to operate through our own efforts without relying on God's strength, we are a lot like this balloon. We move along through life and everything seems to be going okay, until one day we hit a snag. We encounter something that we hadn't planned—something that is completely overwhelming to us—and our strength isn't enough to get us through.

At this point, pop the balloon with the needle (this should get a nice reaction from the group). Now pick up the second balloon with the tape on the end. Continue the lesson by saying, "However, when we rely on God's strength, we are like this balloon." Push the needle through the tap, keeping a good grasp on the needle, and then remove it. Explain that this balloon didn't pop when you poked it with the needle because it was reinforced by tape.

Read the key verse in Matthew 28:20, in which Jesus promises that He will be with each and every one of us for all time. Conclude the session by stating that Jesus will give us strength and reinforce our lives when we rely

on Him. For this reason, we don't have to fear that we will pop like the first balloon when adversity comes our way, because we know that Christ has promised to be with us, and He always keeps His promises to us.

additional verses

Exodus 15:2; 1 Chronicles 16:11; Nehemiah 8:10; Psalms 20:7-8; 27:1; 28:8; 105:4; Daniel 10:18-20; Zechariah 4:6; 2 Corinthians 12:9-10

43

taste and see

key verse

"Taste and see that the Lord is good" (Psalm 34:8).

materials needed

apple, orange, or other edible fruit or food

object lesson

Display the apple or other edible piece of fruit or food, and then tell the following story:

> The tale is told about an important philosopher who traveled the land giving lectures on God, mankind and the meaning of life. At one stop he was talking about God, ridiculing the Bible and Jesus Christ. As he spoke, he challenged anyone to come forward and refute what he said. "Prove me wrong," he proudly huffed. "Prove that Jesus is real."
>
> From the back of the audience, an old man slowly stood and walked forward. The man was eating an orange. The teacher watched the old man approach and chuckled as he thought about how his "wisdom" would destroy anything the naïve old man had to say.
>
> The old man came to the podium. As the teacher and the audience looked on, the old man calmly finished his orange, obviously enjoying every bite. Finally the old man spoke up and said, "Good orange, wasn't it?"
>
> The teacher smirked. "Well, how should I know?" he said. "I didn't try it!"
>
> With that, the old man winked and left the stage. The philosopher and the audience got the message: Don't knock Jesus if you've never tried Him.

Read the key verse in Psalm 34:8, and then ask the group if the apple (or other fruit) that you are holding in your hand tastes good. Tell the

students that there is really no way to know until you try it. Take a bite out of the apple and say, "It tastes good. You see, apples are meant to be enjoyed—not with our eyes or our hands, but with our taste buds."

Discuss how ridiculous it would be to buy an apple and just hang it from your front-room ceiling so everyone could say, "My, what a fine-looking apple." In the same way, it would be silly to pass the apple around at school so that everyone could talk about it and discuss its nature and importance. This is because apples are meant to be eaten.

Explain to the group that this is just the same with our relationship with Christ. Christianity is meant to be experienced—not just talked about or admired. We are to experience our Lord firsthand. No matter how much a person has heard about Jesus, if he or she doesn't sink his or her teeth into Christianity, that person missed the whole point of the gospel.

Conclude the lesson by describing how we can "taste and see." Explain how a person becomes a Christian and the basic things a Christian should be doing to grow spiritually.

additional scriptures

Psalm 119:103; Joshua 24:14-15; Matthew 11:29; John 15:16; Hebrews 6:4-5; 1 Peter 2:2-3

44

that was my year

key verse

"There is a time for everything, and a season for every activity under heaven" (Ecclesiastes 3:1).

materials needed

trophy
bucket
toilet seat
mirror
plant food
candle
junk mail
microwave
oversized pair of jeans (60″ x 30″ works well)
diaper

preparation

Display each of the items on a table. Feel free to add any other creative items to the list.

object lesson

This is a great visual to use for a year-end evaluation/challenge talk to help your students analyze the past year and set a course for the new year ahead.

To begin, use each of the items as a representation of what the students' year might have been like. For example, for the trophy, you could say, "Perhaps you accomplished something really big this year. It was like winning a trophy." For the bucket, you could say, "Or maybe you felt in over your head most of the year, like you were constantly bailing yourself out."

Here are a few additional suggestions for what each of the items might represent:

- *Toilet seat*: Just a bad year all around
- *Mirror*: God taught you something about yourself

spiritual growth

- *Plant food*: You grew spiritually during the year
- *Candle*: You found Christ this year
- *Junk mail:* A lot of hype, but it turned out empty
- *Microwave:* It was really cooking and went by fast
- *Oversized jeans*: A really big year for you
- *Diaper:* It kind of stunk

additional scriptures

Nehemiah 1–2; 1 Corinthians 3:10-15; Philippians 3:13-14; Revelation 21:1-6

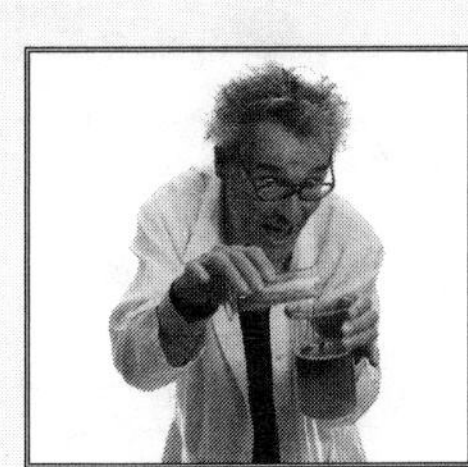

45

what a plant needs to grow

key verses

"Forgetting what is behind and straining toward what is ahead, I press on toward the goal to win the prize for which God has called me heavenward in Christ Jesus" (Philippians 3:13-14).

materials needed

a small house plant
a small pot for the plant
plant food (Miracle-Gro® or another type of plant food)
potting soil
glass of water
gardening trowel, gloves and an apron (for the "dramatic" effect)

object lesson

Begin by stating some comparisons between the plant and the Christian life. (For example, we receive Christ and begin our journey as a small seed that begins to blossom into a plant, but in order for us to continue in our walk with Christ, we need to grow.)

Ask the group members what it would take for the plant to grow properly. As they discuss some of the things that the plant needs to grow, begin repotting the plant in front of the group. As you do this, explain each of the following items and the importance of each item or ingredient in the process:

- For the plant to grow, we need to take action by caring for it, just as we must take care of our walk with Christ.

- Each ingredient we use in repotting the plant is essential for its growth, just as there are ingredients that are essential in helping our relationship with Jesus grow (reading His Word, prayer, fellowship, worship, spiritual disciplines, and so forth).

- Just as we may not see the growth in this plant from day to day, we may not immediately see the growth in our own lives. However, over time we will see the growth and the fruit that it produces!

- When we begin to "outgrow" our environment (become complacent and comfortable), we need to be "repotted" (challenged with a new step of maturity). If we don't move into a new experience, we may become stunted or cease to grow spiritually altogether.

Conclude by summarizing the process of growth: "First, we need to *seed it*—begin our relationship with God. Then we need to *feed it*—take action by caring for our relationship with God every day. Finally, we need to *weed it*—take time to weed out the areas of our lives that need to change."

additional scriptures

1 Corinthians 9:24-25; Colossians 1:28; 3:1-17; James 1:2-4

DISCUSSION STARTERS

discussion \ di-skə-shən \ **1:** consideration of a question in open and usually informal debate **2:** a formal treatment of a topic in speech or writing.

starter \ stär-tər\ **1:** a person who initiates **2:** one who causes something to begin operating **3:** something that is the beginning of a process, activity or series.

Educators often refer to "the teachable moment." It is that special experience in a learning setting when the learners are primed and begging for words of wisdom to spill from your mouth. It is that occasion when the students are so into the program or topic that they would rather sit and listen to you than take a trip to the mall or a movie. It does not happen often in youth ministry, but it is wonderful when it does.

This teachable moment can be manufactured, enabling you to have more opportunities to grab the kids' attention and share with them. It is controlled and directed by you, the leader, but it appears to the kids to be something that just happened. One valuable means by which you can bring such a teaching moment into being is through discussion starters.

A discussion starter is a brief statement that is sometimes weighty, sometimes nonjudgmental, sometimes silly, sometimes poignant, but always interesting enough to promote youth to circle up the wagons and talk. It's that question or comment that somehow capsulizes what is going on and turns it into a relevant discussion.

Try some discussion starters on those way-too-long bus rides, or while sipping a soda, or when you're just with the kids. Learn to manufacture wonderful teaching moments by using discussion starters.

1

key verse

"Be strong and courageous. Do not be terrified; do not be discouraged, for the Lord your God will be with you wherever you go" (Joshua 1:9).

illustration

A woman was once travelling by plane to a conference. Although she was prone to airsickness, she did not take any airsickness pills before the flight, as it was a short trip and she didn't think she would not get sick. Unfortunately, she was wrong—during the flight she became very nauseous.

Fumbling through the seat back in front of her, she found a barf bag and pulled it out. However, she chose not to use it at that time. Instead, she waited patiently for the plane to land.

When the plane arrived at the airport gate, the woman made a mad dash to be the first off the plane. She had to get to a restroom as quickly as possible and then make her connecting flight. As it turned out, the woman had waited too long, and as she walked up the ramp, she vomited on herself and the man who was walking in front of her, ruining his suit.

Flight attendants rushed to help clean them both up. The woman was embarrassed, and she also missed her connecting flight. All this occurred because she did not use the bag that had been provided for her.

discussion questions

1. What is a situation you've been in where you thought you had everything under control, but it turned out that you did not?
2. How would you handle the situation differently now?
3. God has given us many tools to use when we have a crisis or when life is too busy, such as prayer, His Word, Christian friends and mentors. When have you ignored God's tools and resources that could have helped you in a difficult situation?
4. Next time you face a difficult situation, what can you do to remind yourself of God's tools that can help you?

additional scriptures

Romans 15:4; 2 Timothy 3:16-17; 2 Peter 1:3-9

2

a failure to plan

key verse

"'For I know the plans I have for you,' declares the Lord, 'plans to prosper you and not to harm you, plans to give you hope and a future'" (Jeremiah 29:11).

illustration

Each time Mr. Higgins read of a house fire in the newspaper, he mentioned to his wife how important it was to develop and practice a fire escape plan for them and their children. Mrs. Higgins always agreed, noting that they had so much to lose and it was easy to be prepared. Occasionally, the two would draw out on paper or discuss the best ways to escape the house if a fire occurred. However, they never actually tried out the plan. The family moved quite a lot with Mr. Higgins's work, and a new fire plan was necessary with each new home.

Sadly, the Higgins family only truly got serious about a fire plan after their house and possessions were completely lost in a devastating fire. They barely escaped with their lives, and Mr. Higgins was severely burned while trying to find his children and help them escape. Although the family survived, the life-changing injuries to Mr. Higgins and the trauma of this horrifying experience dramatically affected the whole family.

discussion questions

1. How could the Higgins family have been better prepared?
2. What is wrong with an untried plan?
3. How does this story of Mr. Higgins apply to our Christian lives and spiritual growth?
4. In what ways are you like the Higgins family when it comes to your "plan" for growing in Christ? In what ways are you different?
5. What could you do today to ensure that you stick to your plan for reading your Bible, praying and spending time with God each day?

additional verses

Proverbs 16:3; 1 Corinthians 16:13; Hebrews 6:11; Jude 1:3

3

the election

key verse

"Are not two sparrows sold for a penny? Yet not one of them will fall to the ground apart from the will of your Father" (Matthew 10:29).

illustration

Anthony was really bummed. He had long paid his dues to be considered for student government at his high school. His list of credentials was quite impressive: principal's office aide, president of the jazz and art clubs, honor-roll member, marching band treasurer and all-around good guy. He really liked school and invested his time and energy in pursuing his goal of being the senior class president.

And now, after a tough campaign, the vote indicated that Shawna was the new senior class president. He had lost. The disappointment was heightened by the fact that Shawna had been elected because of her popularity. She was cute, very personable and very *uninterested* in the politics of the school. She had run on a whim to receive more attention and had thoroughly trounced Anthony. Perhaps even more disconcerting, Shawna had no idea what the issues and challenges of school leadership were. She would likely do nothing to enhance the overall climate of the school.

Losing the election made Anthony wonder if God really knew what He was doing. He had firmly believed that God was moving him along a path of leadership that would benefit not only the student body, but also the Body of Christ. Now what was happening?

discussion questions

1. What would you tell Anthony if you were his friend?
2. Why would God lead someone to try to reach a goal and then allow such a disappointing result?
3. What are some reasons why God might be holding Anthony back from this leadership position?
4. What kind of leader will Shawna turn out to be? Is the popular vote reliable for good leadership choices?

5. Have you voted for the most popular student when you knew that another candidate would probably be a better leader? If so, why did you vote as you did?

additional verses

Job 42:2; Psalm 145:14; Proverbs 3:5; Romans 8:28

4

is there really any difference?

key verse

"If anyone is ashamed of me and my words, the Son of Man will be ashamed of him when he comes in his glory and in the glory of the Father and of the holy angels" (Luke 9:26).

illustration

Jason was a well-rounded guy and a good kid. He did a little bit of everything. He made good grades, played most sports well and was a member of the school's marching band. He even helped out at a local homeless shelter.

One day at lunch, Jason and some friends were talking about life and what they wanted to do after they graduated. Jason said to his friends, "I think I would like to do some mission work in Juarez, Mexico, where I went last summer."

Jason's friends started laughing and joking with him about how silly that would be. One friend said, "Jason, that sounds like something one of those geeky Christians would say, and you are not one of those." Jason just laughed along with his friends and left without saying another word.

That night, Jason struggled with doubts and questions. Why did his friends not know he was a Christian? Why did they think Christians were geeky? What was a Christian guy supposed to do? Wasn't he different from his friends?

Jason sat down and began to list how he was different from his friends. First, whenever anyone told a dirty joke, he just listened. He never told any dirty jokes himself. Second, he had never copied someone else's homework. In fact, he was usually the nice guy who let others copy his homework. Third, whenever he was at his friends' parties, he never drank alcohol—he only drank soda. Finally, though he had made out with a few girls, he had never gone all the way.

Of course, some might think he had from the way he had left out a few of the details . . .

discussion questions

1. What might be answers to Jason's questions? What conclusion do you think he came to that night about the way he was living as a Christian?
2. Was Jason really any different from his non-Christian friends? If so, how?
3. Did his life reflect the difference God had made in it? Explain.
4. What are some steps that Jason could take to right this situation and to help others see Christ in him?
5. How do you relate to Jason? What steps will you take to make the necessary changes in your lifestyle?

additional scriptures

Matthew 5:14-16; 10:32-33; Mark 8:34-38; Romans 1:16; 10:14-15; Colossians 3:1-10,12-17; 1 Timothy 1:8-9; 1 Peter 3:13-16

5

the love letter

key verse

"Whoever does not love does not know God, because God is love" (1 John 4:8).

illustration

Todd and Sarah were college students who met during summer vacation while working at a resort. They started off by saying hello whenever they saw each other. Todd finally got up the courage to ask Sarah out for a date, and the romance began. Todd and Sarah would spend their days off together at the beach, taking long walks or going out to get something to eat. They were both in love. Yet Todd was shy and had a hard time expressing his feelings to Sarah with words.

The summer quickly passed, and the cool fall breezes meant that it was time for Todd to fly home. Sarah took him to the airport, and they spent a long time embracing each other as tears welled up in their eyes. Would they ever see each other again? Finally, it was time for Todd to board the plane. He pulled an envelope out of his pocket with Sarah's name on it and gave it to her. Then he turned and walked slowly away. Sarah cried as she put the envelope in her purse and headed for her car.

Sarah was terribly depressed. On the way home, she stopped at a restaurant and ordered lunch. Sitting at the table, she took the envelope out of her purse and looked it over, but then quickly put it away when the waitress brought the food. She wasn't sure she wanted to read it anyway. Lunch was okay, but nothing tasted as good anymore now that Todd was gone. If only she could hear his voice right now. But she couldn't.

When Sarah got home, she turned on the television. She couldn't find a program that interested her, but she watched a soap opera anyway. She figured she might as well be depressed by someone else's problems instead of her own. However, no matter what she did, Sarah could not chase away the reality that Todd was gone. She loved him so much. What would she do without him? During a commercial, she remembered the envelope.

She turned off the television and took the letter out of her purse. She looked at the outside of the envelope once again, wondering what Todd might have written. Just then, the shrill ring of the telephone broke the

silence. Putting the envelope down, Sarah answered the phone. It was her friend Willa, asking if Sarah would go to the mall with her. Willa knew that Sarah would be feeling bad, so she figured this would get her mind off of Todd being gone. Knowing she should get out, Sarah agreed to go and glanced at the envelope as she went out the door. *Oh, if we could only be together*, she thought.

Days went by and nothing cheered Sarah up. It was almost like Todd had died. Occasionally, Sarah would pick up the envelope that Todd had addressed to her and look at it, but she never opened it. It just made her sad, and it seemed that something always got in the way. *Why hasn't Todd called me?* Sarah often wondered. *He must not really love me or else he would have called.*

Weeks went by, and Sarah began to resent Todd. *He doesn't care about me*, she thought. *What a jerk I was to believe that he loved me*. She looked for the envelope he had given her and found it under a pile of bills and papers. It was rumpled now—wrinkled and stained by a coffee spill. "Todd, where are you?" she cried as she threw the envelope across the room. It landed in a corner.

Months later, Sarah found the envelope still lying in the corner. She picked it up and put it in the trash. The letter that she never opened from Todd had said:

> Dear Sarah:
>
> Although these words have not yet been said, they have now long been true.
>
> These words will closely bond us although they are few,
>
> They can never be broken, wherever I am, or whatever you do.
>
> My Sarah, my dear Sarah, nothing else matters than this: "I love you."
>
> Will you marry me?
>
> Please reply.
>
> —Todd

discussion questions

1. Describe your feelings about Sarah not opening Todd's letter. What did she miss out on because she did not read it?
2. What were some of the reasons that Sarah gave for not opening Todd's letter? Were these valid reasons? Why or why not?
3. How is this story similar to people who say they want to know God but won't read the Bible?

4. What reasons do people have for not reading the Bible?
5. How can you overcome the obstacles that keep you from reading God's Word?

additional scriptures

Psalms 19:7-10; 119:103,105; Ezekiel 3:3; John 1:1-5,14,18; Colossians 3:16; 2 Timothy 3:16; 1 John 4:9-10

6

the mission trip

key verse

"We all, like sheep, have gone astray, each of us has turned to his own way" (Isaiah 53:6).

illustration

The youth group of First Church boarded the plane for Alaska. It was the most ambitious cross-cultural mission trip they had ever planned. The two weeks they would spend in a remote Native Alaskan village doing evangelism and helping the local pastor repair the church's deteriorating facilities had taken an enormous amount of planning, prayer and training on the part of the students and the adult leaders. The excitement level was high as the plane lifted off, and it remained high the following day as the group boarded smaller bush planes that brought them to their final destination.

On the group's first night in the village, four residents approached a number of the students who were relaxing outside the church building. They asked them why they had come to the village. The students explained who they were and what they hoped to accomplish while they were there. They invited the villagers to come to the evangelistic services that they would be leading later in the week.

The four residents were frankly unimpressed and declined their invitation. They told the student missionaries that from their perspective, the Christian Church had played the major role in destroying their culture, their language, their art and their sense of identity as Alaskan native people. They went on to detail for the students how this had come about, and they even suggested that the group should leave the village earlier than they had planned.

Later that evening, the youth group members discussed whether or not it was appropriate for them to be sharing their faith in a culture they apparently knew little about.

discussion questions

1. How would you summarize the situation that these student missionaries were facing?

2. Were the village residents being fair in their critique of the Christian Church? Explain your answer.
3. Are all things done with sincerity "in the name of Christ" appropriate? Why or why not?
4. Are there some cultures that Christians should leave alone? Why or why not?
5. If you were a leader of the youth group, what would you have said to the students?

additional scriptures

Matthew 28:18-20; Luke 19:10; John 10:10; Acts 3:19

7

the new christian

key verses

"Do you not know that your body is a temple of the Holy Spirit, who is in you, whom you have received from God? You are not your own; you were bought at a price. Therefore honor God with your body" (1 Corinthians 6:19-20).

illustration

Paul was a charming young man who had many friends and a generous heart. Unfortunately, he was also a notorious womanizer. On numerous occasions during any given week, Paul could be seen putting the moves on some young coed. His attractiveness was not only in his handsome looks but also in his appealing personality. Most of the girls, even those who knew his reputation, succumbed to his allure and ended up spending the night at his apartment.

Many of the believers in the small college community in which Paul was a part had been praying for months for him to find Christ. When he eventually did, many were surprised to find that Paul had become a believer through a series of meaningful events and the open sharing of fellow students. When Paul gave his first testimony, he thanked those who had helped him and had prayed for him so diligently. He shared that he had never had any exposure to Christianity before meeting them, and he expressed his gratitude to them for opening his eyes to the gospel.

Everyone rejoiced when Paul became a Christian. However, their joy turned to shock and despair when they discovered that Paul still continued his playboy lifestyle, dating and sleeping with as many young women as he could. The phone lines and concerned whispers buzzed with sadness and a bit too much gossip. What should be done about Paul?

Finally, after many weeks of Paul's continued philandering, one friend in Christ pulled him aside and confronted him on his sexual misbehavior. Stunned, Paul jumped to his feet, his face ablaze with embarrassment. Once calmed, he responded and said, "All of you knew that I had not been raised in the Church. Christianity is new and strange to me. Why did all of you wait so long to tell me that my behavior was wrong?"

discussion questions

1. Did Paul have a valid point with his question?
2. What is the responsibility of the Church to new believers?
3. Have you ever had a problem with an issue of morality and been held accountable for it, even when you had no idea that you were wrong? How did you feel when confronted?
4. What should believers learn from this true story?
5. How would 1 Corinthians 6:18-20 be excellent advice for Paul?

additional scriptures

Jeremiah 7:5; 26:13; Romans 6:1-4; James 1:7-8; Revelation 3:15

8

not my reality

key verse

"Although they knew God, they neither glorified him as God nor gave thanks to him, but their thinking became futile and their foolish hearts were darkened" (Romans 1:21).

illustration

Kim had just attended a high school small-group series on the life of Jesus and was eager to share what she had learned with her friends at school—particularly with those who were not Christians. In the lunchroom one afternoon, she enthusiastically shared what she had learned with Josh. Josh was very attentive to her as she spoke and seemed genuinely excited about everything she had to say.

"That's so cool," he said with genuine sincerity.

"Josh, are you a Christian?" Kim asked.

"Not really," Josh replied. "The Christian thing doesn't really work for me, but I think it's totally cool that it works for you."

Kim thought about this for a moment. "Well," she said, "if the Christian thing doesn't work for you, how come you're excited about it for me?"

Josh considered this question that Kim had asked and then said, "Because even though Christianity is not my reality, I wouldn't want to put you down because it's yours. Everyone's reality is different, and none is better or worse than any other."

The bell for the next period rang, signaling an end to lunch and the conversation with Josh. Kim walked away wondering about some of the things he had said.

discussion questions

1. Have you ever had a conversation like this—from either Kim's or Josh's position? If so, what happened?
2. How would you define the word "reality"?
3. Are there different realities for different people? Why or why not?
4. How can we know what the truth is?

5. Read Romans 1:18-23; 1 Corinthians 1:18-25 and Ephesians 4:17-24. According to Paul, how can believers clearly determine truth from error? What would Paul say to Kim? What would he say to Josh?

additional scriptures

Ecclesiastes 3:11; Romans 1:18-23; 1 Corinthians 1:18-25; Ephesians 4:17-24

a change in behavior

key verse

"An anxious heart weighs a man down, but a kind word cheers him up" (Proverbs 12:25).

illustration

When Jana turned 14, she seemed to become a different person. Before that, she had been a good student who had lots of friends and a great relationship with her parents. Now she was unmotivated in school and generally rude and disrespectful to her mom and dad. Recently, Jana even lost a couple of good friendships because she was so moody and emotional.

discussion questions

1. As a friend of Jana, what might you say to her?
2. In what ways could you encourage her to reach out and let her friends know what she is going through?
3. How could you encourage her to reconnect with her parents?
4. What are a few things Jana or her friends can do to help her overcome her moodiness?
5. What could you say to the friends whom Jana lost because of her moodiness to help them reconnect?

additional scriptures

Ephesians 4:15-16; 6:1; Colossians 3:20; 2 Thessalonians 2:16-17; Hebrews 10:24-25

10

the date

key verse

"Do not lie. Do not deceive one another" (Leviticus 19:11).

illustration

Becky thought that Greg was the best-looking, funniest guy she had ever met. She had not had many dates, but she was hoping for one with Greg. Becky's mom, on the other hand, had told her that she thought Greg was not the right kind of boy to date. He was not a Christian, and Becky had said she was only going to date Christian boys. Yet Becky had convinced herself that because Greg came to church sometimes, this was good enough.

One day, Greg asked Becky to meet him at a nearby park. It wasn't a real date, but it was close enough. It sounded fun and exciting to Becky, but she knew she had to do it without her mom knowing. So, that night she went to spend the night at a friend's house—or so she told her mom.

Becky felt awkward asking her friend to lie to cover for her, so she told her friend that she needed to run to the store for something. Then she went to the park to meet Greg. She had a fun time and got back to the friend's house within a couple of hours. Everything seemed under control.

discussion questions

1. How would you define a lie? When did the lying begin in Becky's case?
2. Why do you think it made Becky feel awkward to ask her friend to lie when she was already lying?
3. How do you think Becky felt while she was telling the lies?
4. How do you think it made others feel when and if they found out they were lied to?
5. Has this ever happened to you? How did it make you feel? How did it affect your relationship with the people involved?

additional scriptures

Psalm 52:2-4; Proverbs 6:16-17; 26:18-19,28; James 3:5-12

11

delinquents or outcasts?

key verse

"Woe to you, teachers of the law and Pharisees, you hypocrites! . . . You have neglected the more important matters of the law—justice, mercy and faithfulness" (Matthew 23:23).

illustration

The older adults in a small, affluent mid-western community reacted with anger when the teenagers in the town became interested in skateboarding and in-line skating. The teens would skate in empty parking lots and streets that were not used much and then congregate in the town square or behind some of the stores. Many adults became upset about this and complained to the police. After many such complaints, the police restricted the teens' skating and accompanying loitering.

One downtown merchant became concerned that the skaters had no place to hang out. He feared that if there weren't some space for them to use, they would resort to mischief out of boredom. So he began to give several of them written permission to use his private business parking lot for skating after hours. He told them to keep the permission letter with them and, if questioned, to simply show it to the police. He believed this would stop any problems between the teens and the officials.

One evening, the skaters were stopped, questioned and finally taken into custody for violating the police order against skating. When they argued they had permission and tried to show their permission slips, the police shouted them down and refused to read the paper. They were taken to the police station, and their parents were called.

These so-called delinquents were all from respectable families, and some were even Christians. None of them had ever caused trouble in the community before.

discussion questions

1. How would you feel if you were one of these skaters?
2. Why might the police act this way toward these teenagers?

3. Look at both sides of the conflict. What are the legitimate concerns and needs of both the adults and the teens?
4. What better plan could be developed in communities where youth and adults clash over leisure space?
5. How might a church become involved in such a matter? Does the church have any place in community disputes such as this?

additional scriptures

Mark 7:9; Luke 18:9; Galatians 5:6; 1 John 5:3-4

12

joint custody

key verse

"If it is possible, as far as it depends on you, live at peace with everyone" (Romans 12:18).

illustration

Mr. and Mrs. Kramer had finally agreed upon joint custody of their three kids after their divorce. It was decided that the children would live with their dad the first and third weeks of the month and with their mom the second and fourth weeks. Both Mr. and Mrs. Kramer lived within the school district boundaries, so the children's attendance would not be affected by the arrangement.

However, what was problematic for the children was dividing their time between the two churches their parents attended. This was especially problematic for the Kramers' son, Lennie, who was active in the youth group of Fellowship Christian Church. This was the church his family had always attended as he was growing up, and his dad still attended. More importantly, it was Lennie's church.

Yet Lennie's mom insisted that he visit the youth group of her new church, Grace Chapel, during the weeks he spent under her care. The youth group was okay, but Lennie was a member of the worship band and a student discipleship leader at his church. He simply did not know how to be active in both groups.

Lennie has since become frustrated with dividing his time between the two churches, and he's now ready to give up and quit both groups.

discussion questions

1. What do you think about the Kramers' arrangements for the kids? Is it a good set-up?
2. Is Lennie's mom being unfair in insisting that he attend Grace Chapel during the weeks he is with her? Why or why not?
3. Is Lennie being rigid and unfair? Should he try to accept both groups? Why or why not?
4. What should Lennie tell his parents?

5. How would you react if this were your life? Is anything in your situation similar to this story?

additional scriptures

Exodus 20:12; Proverbs 17:14; Ephesians 4:3; Hebrews 12:14

13

losing control

key verses

"Get rid of all bitterness, rage and anger, brawling and slander, along with every form of malice. Be kind and compassionate to one another, forgiving each other, just as in Christ God forgave you" (Ephesians 4:31-32).

illustration

Lauren and her mom argued more than most mothers and daughters. Family members told them over and over again that the reason they fought was because they were more alike than they would admit. Neither of them knew how to handle conflict.

Whenever Lauren was angry with her mom, she would scream, "I hate you!" and call her mom terrible names. The problem continued to escalate, until Lauren's mom began to lose her temper at Lauren's outbursts and responded by slapping Lauren in the face. These episodes of Lauren and her mom losing control were becoming more and more frequent.

Lauren was afraid that one day her mother would really hurt her. After her mother hit her, she would usually come back when things calmed down and apologize for losing control. Lauren knew that she shouldn't talk back to her mom, but she also knew that her mom was not right in hitting her.

discussion questions

1. What are the issues in Lauren's and her mom's situation?
2. What does this family need to do?
3. Where is the mom at fault?
4. Where is Lauren at fault?
5. If Lauren came to you, what advice would you give her?

additional scriptures

Psalm 37:8; Proverbs 15:1; Zephaniah 3:17; 1 Peter 5:7

14

no connection

key verse

"He must be hospitable, one who loves what is good, who is self-controlled, upright, holy and disciplined" (Titus 1:8).

illustration

On a recent trip, a youth group member, Doug, had to be physically removed from the vicinity of the soda and candy machines at a gas station because he was attempting to pull them down. He was found in a flurry of kicking, hitting and shoving the machines, and the youth worker, John, had to hold his arms at his sides and pull him from the vending room of the gas station.

Outside, John asked Doug what he was doing. Doug told him that the machine had taken his money, giving him no change and no soda. He admitted that he had momentarily lost his temper and was intent on causing damage to the machine for ripping him off.

As he and John talked, Doug finally admitted that he was upset because his parents had announced to the family that they were splitting up. This came on the same day that he had been cut from the varsity basketball team, flunked a major math test and also had a disagreement with his girlfriend.

Gently, John asked Doug if he was perhaps more upset about the way things were going in life than he was about losing a dollar in the machine. Doug just looked blankly at John and insisted to him that there was no connection.

discussion questions

1. What do you think was really bothering Doug?
2. How often do we take out our anger, failure or helplessness on other things or people that are not the source of our trouble?
3. Why do we react with such aggression when a small frustration ticks us off?
4. Have you ever gone nuts over a small thing? Was it a smoke screen to cover how you felt about something much more serious?

5. Read 1 Peter 5:6-11 and John 14:27; 16:33. What worries, cares or hardships are you facing alone? Would it help to share them with Jesus? Why or why not?

additional scriptures

Psalm 138:7; Isaiah 40:31; John 14:27; 16:33; 1 Peter 5:6-11

15

pizza night

key verse

"Then you will know the truth, and the truth will set you free" (John 8:32).

illustration

Mark's parents had divorced a few years ago, and his life had been in a tailspin ever since the family had broken up. The youth worker in Mark's church group could see that he needed help badly. So he arranged to meet with Mark on a regular basis to help him sort out his problems.

After a few counseling sessions, Mark tearfully admitted that he had been the cause of his parents' divorce. He was certain that his parents had divorced when he was in fifth grade as the result of some bad decision-making on his part. He told the youth worker that he would hold on to that guilt forever.

Gently probing, the youth worker encouraged Mark to share with him the details of how he, as a 10-year-old, could in one single situation cause something as huge as a divorce. With tears in his eyes, Mark explained to the youth worker that his father had announced he would be leaving the family on the Monday after Mark had missed the family weekly pizza night on Friday.

In amazement, the youth worker listened as Mark told bits of his story to him. Apparently, for years the family had eaten pizza on Friday nights prior to attending various high school sporting events. Mark's dad worked in the school's athletic department. On that particular Friday night, a friend of the family had invited Mark to dinner, and for the first time in his young life, he missed the family pizza gathering. Three days later, his dad left.

The facts were obvious to Mark: Dad had left because he had broken tradition. The family breakup was all Mark's fault as far as he was concerned.

discussion questions

1. Was the divorce Mark's fault?
2. Why would Mark believe that it was his fault?
3. What do you think really happened?

4. Have any of you believed that you were the cause of your parents' arguments or their divorce?
5. Read John 8:32. How might we allow Christ to show us the truth that we might erase our erroneous beliefs?

additional scriptures

Psalm 85:11; John 16:13; Philippians 3:14; 2 John 4

16

prom night sleepover

key verse

"Flee the evil desires of youth, and pursue righteousness, faith, love and peace, along with those who call on the Lord out of a pure heart" (2 Timothy 2:22).

illustration

Prom night was just two days away. For some weeks, Stacey had been pleading with her parents to allow her to attend a co-ed sleepover after the prom, but it seemed she was making little progress. She had tried every argument she could think of to convince her parents that it would be all right—and then some.

"But, Mom, everybody is going to sleep over at Ricky's house after the homecoming dance."

"Ricky's mom and dad will chaperone."

"It's mostly the church youth-group kids who will be there."

"We won't be drinking or having sex."

"Don't you trust me?"

"Everyone else's parents are letting them sleep over."

"You and Dad are so old-fashioned."

discussion questions

1. What do you think about Stacey's dilemma?
2. What do you think is the main issue that Stacey's parents had about the sleepover?
3. Were Stacey's parents right in telling her that she couldn't go to the sleepover?
4. What advice would you give to Stacey?
5. What advice would you give to Stacey's parents?

additional scriptures

Deuteronomy 4:9; Proverbs 15:1; 25:11; Ephesians 6:1; Colossians 3:20

17

sound-system wars

key verse

"Let your conversation be always full of grace, seasoned with salt, so that you may know how to answer everyone" (Colossians 4:6).

illustration

The sound system of Kevin's dreams was sitting there right in front of him. It had everything—all the bells and whistles. Kevin would have never dreamed in a million years that his parents would have bought him something like this. *My parents are the best*, Kevin thought.

"Happy birthday, dear," Kevin's mom said, affection oozing from her tone of voice.

"Son, we also bought you the best earphones we could find," Kevin's dad added. "When your mother and I are around, please use them."

Man, I knew there was a catch, Kevin thought. To him, it was like being given a sports car but told that you couldn't drive it faster than 35 mph. It just wasn't right.

Within three months, the sound-system wars had already inflicted serious damage on the family's relationships. Every morning, Kevin would get up and turn on the system. He only knew one volume setting: *loud*. He needed the noise to help him wake up. Kevin's dad was just the opposite. He liked to ease into each new day with a cup of coffee, his newspaper and some peace and quiet.

Each day, the same scenario seemed to play itself out. When Kevin was in the shower, his dad would go into Kevin's bedroom and turn off the system. When Kevin got back to his room, he would get angry that someone had turned the music off, slam his door and turn the music back on—just a bit louder to make his point. His mom would then go to Kevin's bedroom, knock on the door and yell, "Turn it down, honey! Do you hear me? Turn it down!"

Kevin could hear his mother, but he ignored her. *God, why did You give me parents like this?* He would often wonder.

One day Kevin came home from school, and as usual he looked forward to kicking back and relaxing to some good music. His parents were always at work in the afternoon, so this was *his* time. But when he walked into his bedroom, he couldn't believe his eyes. The sound system was gone.

Kevin was furious. He went to his parents' room, unhooked their television from the cable, took it and hid it in the attic. *Two can play at this game*, Kevin thought. Then he went back to his room and dreamed how he could trade his parents in for a new set.

When both his parents had come home from work, Kevin stormed out of his room and made his grand entrance into the kitchen. "What do you think you are doing?" he yelled. "You had no right to go into my room without my permission, and you have absolutely no right to take my property! You thieves! Give me my stereo back!"

Kevin's mom responded as calmly as she could. "Sweetie, calm down," she said. "We have every right to do what we did. We are your parents. You live in our house and you live under our rules. We love you, and we are trying to teach you responsibility."

"Give it back!" Kevin screamed.

Kevin's dad was not nearly as calm as his mother. "Son, you are so ungrateful!" he exclaimed, pointing his finger at Kevin. "We gave you that sound system out of the kindness of our hearts, and you abused that kindness. Do you hear me? We've asked you to be considerate. Then we told you what we expected from you. We told you that if you didn't respect our requests, we'd have to do something that you wouldn't like! Yet you have consistently ignored our wishes!"

"You had no right to take it!" Kevin again screamed. "I want it—"

"We will not give the system back!" Kevin's dad yelled. "In fact, we cannot give it back, because . . . we SOLD it! We even talked to Pastor Steve about this. He told us that if you wouldn't obey us, we were doing the right thing by selling the system!"

Kevin's mind was racing. He couldn't believe what he was hearing. Even the youth pastor had sold him out. He turned away and walked toward the back door. When he reached it, he looked back at his parents as he opened the door. Firmly but calmly he said, "I want it back. Oh, and by the way, Mommy and Daddy, have fun watching TV tonight."

With that parting shot, Kevin walked out and slammed the door.

discussion questions

1. Which of the characters in the story do you consider to be the most at fault in this situation? Why?
2. What could have been done in this situation to prevent the conflict from becoming so severe?

3. Was it appropriate for the youth pastor to get involved? Why or why not?
4. What are some ways to express disagreement with a parent in a way that still shows honor and respect?
5. What steps can be taken to improve communication between parents and their children?

additional scriptures

Proverbs 12:18; Ephesians 6:1-3; Philippians 2:4; Colossians 3:12-17,20-21

18

the collision

key verse

"Who shall separate us from the love of Christ? Shall trouble or hardship or persecution or famine or nakedness or danger or sword?" (Romans 8:35).

illustration

Phil was to be one of the speakers on Youth Sunday at church. He had committed to sharing his testimony about his faith in Christ and how Jesus had helped him in times of trouble and stress. However, when it came time to start the service, the sanctuary was packed and Phil had not yet shown up. A quick call to Phil's house had not brought any answers. No one had seen him.

The youth group had no choice but to move on without him. Then, between the first and second services, while the participants were enjoying donuts and tweaking their parts for a better presentation, Phil walked in. It was obvious from his face that something was very, very wrong.

Phil was a new driver. It had snowed all through the night, and on his way to the service, Phil had slid through a stop sign and collided with another car. He had received a few bumps and bruises, had gotten a ticket, and his car was a total loss. However, what he had actually lost was far more significant.

Phil was angry with God that he had had this accident on the very day that he was going to stand before the congregation and share about his faith. He felt that God had let him down, and he told the other participants that he would be a hypocrite if he were to now get up there in front of the congregation and share what he had written. With anger in his voice and a tear sliding down his cheek, Phil admitted that the accident had caused a great rift between him and God.

discussion questions

1. How would you feel if you were in Phil's shoes?
2. Was Phil being fair in his thinking? Why do bad things happen to Christians, especially when they are trying to serve God?
3. How do you think this accident will affect Phil's faith in the long run?

4. Could you have talked about your faith in God if you had been Phil? Why or why not?
5. Read Psalm 55:1-8. Have you ever felt like Phil and wondered where God was when you were facing tough times?

additional scriptures

Psalm 55:1-8; Romans 15:4; 2 Corinthians 4:8-11; James 1:12-18

19

suicide note

key verse

"Cast all your anxiety on him because he cares for you" (1 Peter 5:7).

illustration

Mrs. Centeno stared down at the piece of paper that she held in front of her. "I hate my family, I hate my church, I hate life," the note read. "I want to die—I've even thought about ways I would kill myself."

Mrs. Centeno had intercepted this note from Sara, one of her third-period students, who was passing it to one of her friends named Mark. Mrs. Centeno was alarmed by what she read and knew that she had to report her potential suicide threat to the authorities. *What could have caused her to become so depressed that she wanted to take her own life?* she wondered.

Later, Mrs. Centeno asked Sara to stay after class. When they were alone, she asked Sara if she had written the note. Sara admitted that she had, but she said that she had just been blowing off some steam to her friend Mark—she didn't really mean what she had written. She begged Mrs. Centeno not to tell her parents about the note, saying that it was all just a misunderstanding.

Mrs. Centeno was concerned and wanted Sara to get the help that she needed.

discussion questions

1. If you were Mrs. Centeno, what would you do in this situation?
2. If you were Sara's friend Mark, what would you do?
3. Do you believe Sara's claim that this was just a misunderstanding? Why or why not?
4. What would be the consequences for Sara if Mrs. Centeno were to tell her parents and the school authorities?
5. How could Psalm 139 offer hope to Sara?

additional scriptures

Nehemiah 9:6; Psalm 139; Nahum 1:7; 1 Corinthians 10:13

20

that sinking feeling

key verse

"But when he saw the wind, he was afraid and, beginning to sink, cried out, 'Lord, save me!' " (Matthew 14:30).

illustration

It had been a long day. Jesus had just performed the miracle of feeding the 5,000, and He now wanted to go up on a mountainside by Himself to pray. So He dismissed the crowd and instructed His disciples to get into a boat and row across the Sea of Galilee to the other side.

When evening came, Jesus was there alone on the mountainside. As He looked down, He could see that the disciples' boat was now a considerable distance away from the shore. He also saw that it was being buffeted by the waves that had been kicked up by the strong winds.

At around three in the morning, Jesus began walking out to them across the sea. When the disciples saw Him, they were afraid and cried out, "It is a ghost!" But Jesus told them to calm down and take courage, for it was Him. "Don't be afraid," He said.

Peter was not completely convinced. "Lord, if it's You," he said, "tell me to come to You on the water."

"Come," said Jesus.

So Peter climbed out of the boat and set his foot down on the water. The footing was solid, so he continued out of the boat and began to make his way toward Christ. However, the wind was still howling all around him, and Peter began to be afraid that he wouldn't make it all the way to Jesus. When he began to doubt and take his eyes off of Jesus, he also began to sink. "Lord, save me!" he cried.

Jesus reached out and caught him. "Why did you doubt?" He asked (see Matthew 14:22-33).

discussion questions

1. What trial are you currently facing? What situation in your life seems as impossible as walking on water?
2. If you were absolutely convinced that Jesus would enable you to make it through this situation, what would you do to face it head-on?

3. Notice that as long as Peter kept his eyes focused on Jesus, he was able to stay on top of the water, but as soon as he turned his attention to his circumstances, he began to sink. What makes it difficult to keep your eyes focused on Jesus?
4. What can you do to stay focused on Jesus?
5. Do you believe that Jesus will always be there to catch you when you feel yourself begin to sink?

additional scriptures

Genesis 22:1-14; 1 Chronicles 5:20; Proverbs 14:12; Isaiah 26:3-4; John 15:4-8

21

trauma from terrorism

key verses

"God is our refuge and strength, an ever-present help in trouble. Therefore we will not fear, though the earth give way and the mountains fall into the heart of the sea, though its waters roar and foam and the mountains quake with their surging" (Psalm 46:1-3).

illustration

September 11, 2001, is a day that will never be forgotten. On this day, Carolyn and Jason were standing outside the high school library at their school in Montclair, New Jersey, just across the water from New York City. Carolyn looked up and actually saw the first plane fly into the first of the World Trade Center towers. As they watched in disbelief, another plane dove into the second tower. Jason and Carolyn stood with many of their classmates and watched in horror as both buildings tumbled to the ground.

Carolyn went into a state of shock. Even as the months passed, pushing the horrific tragedy further into the past, she found herself unable to bounce back from the events she had witnessed. She drifted into a state of deep depression and found it hard to even be alone in her own house. Whereas she once used to love looking at the New York City skyline—it was her favorite view in the world—she now found the sight just made her more depressed. She began to have trouble sleeping, and even her faith in God was shaken.

Like Carolyn, Jason was saddened by what had happened on September 11, 2001. Unlike Carolyn, however, Jason's sadness was added to by his having lost a cousin on the ninety-third story of the South Tower on that day. Yet despite his personal loss, after the attacks he seemed to become stronger in his faith and more deliberate about building special family memories. In all respects, he appeared to be much more resilient than Carolyn.

Both Carolyn and Jason are involved in the same youth group.

discussion questions

1. What advice would you have for Jason?
2. What advice would you have for Carolyn?
3. If Carolyn came to you and asked, "Why would God allow something like this to happen?" what might you say to her?
4. Read Isaiah 45:6-7; Lamentations 3:37-38 and Romans 8:28. How do you reconcile what happened on 9-11 and what God says in these passages?
5. What does it mean that "God is in control" or that He is "sovereign"?

additional scriptures

Psalm 55:22; Isaiah 45:6-7; Lamentations 3:37-38; Romans 8:28

22

a very bad day

key verse

"Give thanks in all circumstances, for this is God's will for you in Christ Jesus" (1 Thessalonians 5:18).

illustration

In 1976, Bob Finnegan, a 22-year-old Irishman, was crossing the busy Falls Road in Belfast when he was struck by a taxi and flung over its roof. The taxi drove away, and as Finnegan lay stunned in the road, another car ran into him, rolling him into the gutter. It too drove on. When a group of onlookers gathered to examine the unfortunate Irishman, a delivery van plowed through the crowd, leaving in its wake three injured bystanders and an even more battered Bob Finnegan. When a fourth vehicle came along, the crowd wisely scattered, and only one person was hit: Bob Finnegan. In the span of just two minutes, Finnegan suffered a fractured skull, a broken pelvis, a broken leg and other injuries. He later recovered from his injuries.

discussion questions

1. What was God's part in this particular incident? Was God responsible for what happened to Bob Finnegan?
2. What was Bob Finnegan's part in these events?
3. Where is God in the midst of our bad days?
4. Do you ever have days when it seemed that everything was against you? How do you handle those times?
5. How can you give thanks to God even in the worst of circumstances?

additional scriptures

Deuteronomy 31:8; Romans 8:31-39; 1 Corinthians 10:13; 2 Corinthians 4:7-11

23

a bad influence

key verse

"Dear friend, do not imitate what is evil but what is good. Anyone who does what is good is from God. Anyone who does what is evil has not seen God" (3 John 1:11).

illustration

Bob, a youth pastor, thought the guys in his high school youth group were finally getting their act together. They had actually taken strides to welcome others into the group and were trying to get to know the new people who were attending.

Bob thought it was an especially good sign when he noticed three of the guys in his regular youth group—all professing Christians and from solid Christian backgrounds—welcoming a new student named Mike into their group of friends.

Mike had begun attending church because his mother had found religion and hoped that her son would also benefit. Up to this point in his life, Mike hadn't really heard much about (or at least paid attention to) who Jesus was. However, Pastor Bob was encouraged that Mike was open to hearing and talking about Jesus, and he thought that the guys in the youth group would be a great influence for Christ to him.

About a month later, these four young men—led by one of the youth-group guys—were arrested on felony charges after discharging explosives and lighting gasoline around a disliked teacher's home. Apparently, the three youth-group guys had started to do a series of random pranks around the neighborhood, which had escalated into acts of vandalism and arson. And they had taken Mike along for the ride.

Mike cooperated with the police, and after his arrest it was determined that he had not been significantly involved in the crimes. It seemed to the police that he had innocently gotten involved with the wrong people—in this case, members of Bob's youth group—and he was cleared of all charges.

Mike never returned to the church. Bob tried to contact him, but he never returned his phone calls.

discussion questions

1. What are your thoughts about this story?
2. Why do you think Mike cut his connection with the church and with Pastor Bob?
3. What responsibilities do Christian students have in supporting and building up other Christian students?
4. What are our responsibilities as Christians to students who are not yet believers?
5. How can you be a good influence on those around you?

additional scriptures

Matthew 18:6-9; Romans 14:13; 15:1-2; 1 Corinthians 10:24,32-33; Philippians 2:4

24

the good samaritan

key verse

" 'Love the Lord your God with all your heart and with all your soul and with all your strength and with all your mind'; and, 'Love your neighbor as yourself' " (Luke 10:27).

illustration

One day, a man was walking from Jerusalem to Jericho. The journey was long, and he was hot. He got so tired that he sat down on a rock. While he was resting, some robbers who were lurking nearby spotted him.

"Let's jump him," one of the robbers said.

"Yeah! Let's jump him!" the other robber said. "We'll steal all of his money and beat the snot out of him too!"

So the robbers crept up behind the man. They knocked him off of the rock, attacked him and stole all of his stuff. Then they left him for dead.

The man was terribly beat up. He lay there beside the road, drifting in and out of consciousness, for hours. He moaned in agony from his injuries.

Luckily, a priest happened to walk down the road that day. When he saw the man lying unconscious, he stopped. Standing over the man, he yelled out, "Why don't these homeless people get jobs like everyone else?" He folded his arms and threw back his head in disgust. Then he carefully walked over to the other side of the road, passing by the wounded man.

A little bit later, another religious man, a Levite, showed up. When he came to the wounded man, he found him awake but still groaning because he was in pain. The Levite got down on his knees beside the hurt man. Then, picking up the wounded man's head, he cradled it in his hands and said, "Quit groaning! You're making a scene!"

"Please help me," the hurting man gasped.

"I'm sorry," the Levite replied, "but I just can't. I've got a 2:30 appointment in Jericho to give some money to the poor, and I can't be late." With that, the Levite dropped the man's head to the ground. He started walking away, but then stopped and turned back to the man. "Oh," he said, "I almost forgot to tell you: God loves you, and so do I." With that he turned and walked away.

A little while later, a Samaritan was traveling down the road on his donkey. When he saw the wounded man, he got off his donkey and kneeled down beside him. His heart went out to the man. So he lifted the man onto his donkey and led him to a nearby inn, where he and the innkeeper laid him on the bed in his room.

The next morning, the Samaritan went to the innkeeper and said, "Hey, here's my American Express card. Please take good care of my friend in the room. Whatever he needs, just give it to him and charge it to my card" (see Luke 10:30-35).

discussion questions

1. How can you influence someone else's life by the way you love and serve them?
2. In what ways are you sometimes like the priest when it comes to caring for those in need? In what ways are you like the Levite?
3. What makes it difficult to demonstrate love by serving others?
4. How is it possible to love people you don't even like?
5. What are some specific ways in which you can demonstrate love to people in your life during the next week?

additional scriptures

Luke 6:27-36; 10:25-37; James 1:27; 2:14-17; 1 John 3:18

25

the invisible homeless

key verse

"Religion that God our Father accepts as pure and faultless is this: to look after orphans and widows in their distress" (James 1:27).

illustration

Emily and her youth group were planning on taking a missions trip to Puerto Rico. They had heard reports that the government had taken care of the homeless problem and that the country had completely achieved proper housing for its people. They had even seen American newspaper reports on how the government was making great advances in solving the problem of homelessness in San Juan, the country's capital city and largest municipality. However, when Emily and her youth group arrived and began to tour the city, they immediately noticed a man sleeping in a doorway in an alley. His only blanket was a stained piece of cardboard.

By the week's end, Emily and her group had seen dozens and dozens of homeless people sleeping in a park not far from the mayor's home. The group's hosting pastor said that the city officials would frequently do a mass roundup and drive the homeless out of the city into other communities. It would take about a week for them to walk back into town.

In another major city, a suit had been brought against the local officials for spending money to hide the homeless before a political convention was held in the city. The homeless argued that the huge sums of money could have been better spent on providing some kind of relief housing for them rather than rounding them up and bussing them beyond the city limits or making mass arrests.

discussion starters

1. Have you ever seen homeless people? What were they like? Were you afraid of them? Did you need to be afraid?
2. Do you think the government officials mentioned in this story were justified in removing the homeless from their cities? Why or why not?

3. Do you ever help homeless people? If so, how?
4. What do your parents think about the homeless problem? What does your church feel about the problem? What is your family or church doing to address and solve the problems of the homeless?
5. If you were asked to develop solutions to the homeless problem, what would your plan be?

additional scriptures

Exodus 22:21-22; 23:6; Leviticus 19:14-15; Deuteronomy 15:7-8; Psalm 41:1; Ecclesiastes 5:8; Jeremiah 22:3; Galatians 2:10; 6:9

26

scam artist?

key verse

"Speak up and judge fairly; defend the rights of the poor and needy" (Proverbs 31:9).

illustration

A scruffy-looking man approached Carol and began to talk to her. Although his appearance made her uncomfortable, she tried to listen as the man told her about his hard luck and asked for a few bucks. Her leaning was to give the money to him. However, as she was reaching for her purse, her friend Sean whispered to her that this guy was probably a big-time drug user and that he would only use the money to buy drugs.

The desperate man seemed sincere as he told Carol that he was hungry and would only use the money for food. He had to eat. Noticing Carol's Bible, he reminded her that Jesus helped the poor. Carol glanced at her Bible and then into the eyes of the man. Sean tugged at her arm.

In a flash of movement, Carol took five dollars from her pocket and thrust it into the man's hands. She asked him not to buy drugs with it and to please use it for food. The man's eyes at first showed surprise, and then despair. He became fidgety, hurriedly thanked her, and then asked Carol to pray for him as he quickly walked down the street.

discussion questions

1. Where do you think this man went with Carol's money?
2. What would you have done if you were Carol?
3. Was Sean being fair?
4. Do you think the man was manipulating Carol unfairly by taking note of her Bible?
5. The world is filled with sad stories and hurting people. What is the best way for us to be supportive of them while not feeding their problems?

additional verses

Job 30:25; Psalms 9:9; 113:7; Proverbs 13:23; 14:21; 28:27; 29:7; Isaiah 61:1; 1 John 3:17-18

27

the betrayal

key verse

"Even my close friend, whom I trusted, he who shared my bread, has lifted up his heel against me" (Psalm 41:9).

illustration

Ron and Troy grew up together. They have been close friends for years, and they always hang out together on Friday nights. On one particular Friday, the two had made plans to go to a youth group event at Troy's church. The event was called "Mystery Night," with the mystery being that the youth leaders hadn't told anyone in the youth group where they would be going or what they would be doing.

On Friday, Ron called Troy to say that he was not feeling well and that Troy would have to go to the event by himself. "I'm sorry," he said, "but I'll see you on Sunday—hopefully."

So Troy went to the Mystery Night event by himself. It wasn't too bad, however, because he had lots of other friends in the youth group who were all there. The group ended up going bowling and then afterward to a local pizza place. Once they arrived, Troy and his other friends sat down at a table.

When Troy looked across the room, he was shocked to see Ron sitting with some other friends from school. They were laughing, and they all looked to be having a great time. Ron certainly didn't look like he had been feeling ill.

Suddenly, Ron turned his head and saw Troy staring at him. Busted!

discussion questions

1. Why do you think Ron deceived his friend Troy?
2. If this happened to you, how would you react to Ron's deception?
3. How might this incident change your relationship with Ron?
4. Now change roles. If you were Ron, what would you do?
5. What would Jesus want you to do in this situation?

additional scriptures

Matthew 6:14-15; 7:1-5; 18:15,21-22; Romans 2:1-3; Colossians 3:13-14

28

a celebration denied

key verse

"I know, my God, that you test the heart and are pleased with integrity" (1 Chronicles 29:17).

illustration

The youth at church camp were engaging in the most anticipated event of the week. As usual, the counselors had come up with a great group game and things were going well. The campers were having a fabulous time in the highly active contest.

One of the counselors had made a deal with a rival cabin's team that he would submit to a cream pie in the face if his team lost. This challenge only heightened the fun and made the game more intense. To the delight of the counselor, it looked as if he was going to avoid the consequence of the challenge.

With victory all but assured, the counselor lightheartedly tormented his opponents with whipped cream, shaving cream and other messy gunk. All the students were loving it. They were taking it as it was intended—in fun.

However, the tide changed and the counselor's team unexpectedly lost the challenge. As the winners came after him with cream pies, the counselor fled to his cabin and locked himself in, refusing to allow the winning team their victory celebration. They group waiting for the counselor outside his cabin began to get angry. Eventually, the director had to break up the group because they were close to damaging camp property.

The counselor returned to the group later that day during a presentation by a guest speaker. But by this point, the damage had been done. The counselor had given his word and broken it, and there was nothing anyone could do to restore the spirit of camp fun.

discussion questions

1. Why was this disappointment such a big deal to the students?
2. Did the counselor break the group's trust? Why or why not?
3. What was it about the counselor's broken promise that bothered the teenagers the most?

4. How important is a promise made in fun?
5. How would you have handled the situation if you were the counselor? The director of the camp? One of the disappointed winners?

additional scriptures

Job 27:5; Psalm 25:21; Proverbs 10:9; 11:3; 2 Corinthians 8:21; Titus 2:7-8

dismembered dolls

key verse

"Don't let anyone look down on you because you are young, but set an example for the believers in speech, in life, in love, in faith and in purity" (1 Timothy 4:12).

illustration

An elderly woman gave the youth group a box full of old, used plastic dolls from the 1970s. She believed the kids would like them and asked the youth leader to give them out. When the youth leader looked into the box, she discovered it was filled with the old Troll dolls—the plastic dolls with long, wispy hair dyed in bright colors.

The youth leader gave the dolls as goofy prizes after the game time at the next youth meeting. The girls were really excited. The boys were somewhat skeptical, but they played along. The leader told the students how these prizes had come to the group and mentioned the name of the woman who had donated them.

A little while later, one young woman came up to the youth leader to tell her that some of the boys were dismembering the dolls. She was very upset and disquieted, and she told the leader that she thought the boys' actions were disrespectful to the spirit of the donation. The boys, on the other hand, maintained that they had been given these prizes to do with them as they wished.

discussion questions

1. Was it okay for the boys to dismember the dolls, or was their behavior disrespectful?
2. How would you have felt if you were the elderly woman who had donated the dolls to the youth group and you discovered that the dolls were being dismembered?
3. What should the youth leader say to the young woman who was upset by the boys' actions?
4. What actions, if any, should the leader take with regard to the boys?

5. Was this a legitimate complaint? When you receive a gift, do you feel free to do with it exactly as you wish? Why or why not?

additional scriptures

Psalm 71:7; John 15:13; Philippians 3:13; Titus 2:7

30

key verses

"If you put away the sin that is in your hand and allow no evil to dwell in your tent, then you will lift up your face without shame; you will stand firm and without fear" (Job 11:14-15).

illustration

Melissa was only too happy to assist her father in going through the inventory in their restaurant before the new owners took over. The sale of the family business meant that they would spend more time together. In addition, Mom had made such a great deal on the sale that it would ensure Melissa's and her sister's chances to attend college.

While Melissa was working alone in the basement, she came across some wonderful mugs. They were handmade and glazed and had a beautiful swirling decoration in her favorite shade of blue. Melissa pictured the mugs on her bookshelf at college and decided that she would take them for herself. *After all*, she reasoned, *the new owners won't need them, because they aren't actually used in the restaurant.* She wrapped each mug carefully in newspaper, slipped the mugs into her backpack and finished her tasks.

A few weeks later, Melissa's father grumbled candidly to the whole family at the dinner table that his restaurant staff had ripped him off. He felt that he had been fair to them, generous in his wages and had openly allowed his Christian values to guide him in his dealings with his employees. Now they had robbed him, and he felt hurt.

"What was stolen?" asked Tammy, the youngest daughter.

"A set of mugs that were made for me by my old army buddy," her father replied. "He gave them to me just before he died. It is the only thing that I have to remember him by, and now they are gone."

The family ate the rest of the meal in silence.

Later in her room, Melissa cried into her pillow. What should she do? She did not know that the mugs were her father's. He would never suspect that she took them. How could she be so stupid and hurt her dad in this way?

discussion questions

1. What would you do if you were in Melissa's position?
2. Did Melissa actually steal the mugs, or was it just a misunderstanding?
3. What might happen if Melissa just kept quiet about the missing mugs?
4. How might this event harm Melissa's relationship with her dad?
5. How might this situation be resolved?

additional scriptures

Joshua 7:1-26; Proverbs 28:13; Ezekiel 18:21-22; Luke 15:7

31

playing by different standards

key verse

"Whoever can be trusted with very little can also be trusted with much, and whoever is dishonest with very little will also be dishonest with much" (Luke 16:10).

illustration

Tony and Ellen were in love. Their friends and family teased them by saying their love was just "puppy love," because they were only in high school. They would reply with good humor that puppy love was good for the two of them, because they *were* puppies.

Nearly everyone appreciated the maturity of Ellen and Tony's relationship. Teachers, friends and even their pastor mentioned that the couple's relationship was based on trust, commitment and respect. They were not inappropriately affectionate in public, and they tried to center their dating relationship in Christ. Most agreed it was a dating relationship to hold up as an example to others.

However, Tony's non-Christian parents were not so supportive of his time with Ellen. They constantly tried to control his time, and they often said unkind things about Ellen. This saddened Tony, but he prevailed in good spirit.

The crushing blow came when Tony's dad said that Tony could no longer go to church youth group with Ellen. "Why don't you and your girlfriend go out like other kids?" he said. "You only go to church—no movies, no late-night partying, nothing exciting or fun." Then it hit Tony. His father was embarrassed and perhaps convicted by Tony's moral and pure lifestyle. He wanted his son to go out boozing, not praying, and he was afraid Tony was wasting the best years of his life.

Tony realized that if he played by his dad's standards, then his dad had no problems with him dating Ellen. So Tony began lying, telling his dad that he and Ellen had gone to a wild party or to the movies or to the park. As a result, he received no more complaints from his dad.

Tony hated to lie, but it seemed to be the only way for him to see Ellen. She was not aware of his lies and thought everything was going well. Finally, under strong conviction, Tony suggested to Ellen that they drive through the places he was telling his parents they were visiting on the way to church youth group. The request was so strange that Ellen probed Tony for his reasons. Tony then told her of his father's disappointment and how he was trying to appease his dad by lying about going to undesirable activities and places. He rationalized that if they drove through the places he claimed they were going, it wouldn't really be a lie.

discussion questions

1. What do you think about Tony's solution? Should Tony have conformed to his father's wishes, or is it okay for him to lie for a good reason?
2. What might happen if Tony's parents find out he is lying?
3. How would you react if you were Ellen?
4. What should Ellen and Tony do at this point? Should Tony continue to lie so that they can stay together, or should they break up?
5. What are some other possible solutions to Tony and Ellen's dilemma?

additional scriptures

Proverbs 12:5; Psalm 119:160; Micah 6:12-13; Matthew 15:19; 1 Timothy 1:19

32

stealing sheep

key verse

"So I strive always to keep my conscience clear before God and man" (Acts 24:16).

illustration

After many years of doing nothing together, the youth workers and pastors in a major city decided to band together to promote a combined concert and mission program. Although the pastors came from different branches of Christianity, they had placed their differences on a back burner to make certain the event would honor the unity of the Body of Christ and glorify God. For the first time ever, the teenagers in this community were able to see that many students at their schools were also believers. It was an exciting time for the leaders and students alike.

Just before the event, the students from Faith Church began mingling with some of the teenagers from the other churches in the city. They also began passing out small packets of reading material. Sara, a leader in her youth group at Grace Fellowship, was given a packet. The guy who handed it to her asked her not to read it until she returned home, but he was so cute that Sara could not resist. When she opened the packet, she discovered that it was an invitation to visit Faith Church. Listed were the special youth events, Bible study schedules, church worship times and a coupon to join the kids from Faith Church at a midnight movie party at the mall. The youth group had rented the theater for a private invitation-only showing of a major movie that all of the kids were talking about.

Sara was shocked. The youth group of Faith Church was using the joint youth event to steal sheep from the other church's youth groups. With sadness, Sara went in search of her youth pastor.

discussion questions

1. Are the students and leaders of Faith Church being honorable or dishonorable?
2. What is wrong with this evangelism tactic? Is Faith Church playing fair, or is this being done in bad taste?

3. Have you ever seen a similar situation in your area? What happened?
4. How would you feel if such an effort by another church suddenly cleaned out your youth group? What if some of the students who left to attend the other church accepted the Lord or became more disciplined Christians as a result of the switch?
5. Do churches have an obligation to respect other ministries and not try to grow by "stealing sheep"?

additional scriptures

Psalm 51:6; Proverbs 4:23-27; 1 Corinthians 13:6; 2 Corinthians 4:1-2; Colossians 3:9-10

33

date rape

peer pressure & sexuality

key verse

"Have nothing to do with the fruitless deeds of darkness, but rather expose them" (Ephesians 5:11).

illustration

Ashley was popular in school, active in church and growing in Christ. One summer, she met a boy named Jason at a church camp and fell madly in love with him. Jason was a year older than Ashley and was on the high school basketball team. Soon, they were going out nearly every weekend.

Ashley loved everything about Jason. He was cute, athletic, exciting and smart, and he had a great personality and was a lot of fun. But from the beginning, Ashley felt torn. Jason wasn't a bad guy, but he didn't share some of Ashley's values. He struggled with his faith, and he liked to party. He would invite Ashley to attend his basketball games, and afterward they would go to parties where beer flowed freely. Jason would sometimes join in the drinking, though she never actually saw him get drunk like the others. He seemed to drink just to be sociable, and he always treated her well—never teasing her or allowing others to tease her about not drinking. Yet she always felt uncomfortable about the things that went on at these parties.

Jason was having an awesome year in basketball. His high school team was undefeated and made it to the finals. Ashley got special permission from her parents to attend the final game, even though it was in another city 20 miles away. She cheered as loud as the rest of the fans when the team won 103-101 in overtime. Everyone went to a pizza place to celebrate, but then most of Jason's friends ended up at a motel. Ashley didn't want to go, but Jason insisted. "Just for a little while, please!" he said. Ashley gave in and agreed to go.

Jason was stoked about his part in the championship win. At the pizza place, Ashley noticed that he seemed to be drinking more than usual and that he was getting drunker by the minute. Ashley refused the beer that was offered to her, but she did drink a couple of sodas that Jason handed her. After a while she began to feel kind of weird and dizzy, so she decided to go outside.

The next thing Ashley knew, she was waking up in the back of her car in the motel parking lot. As she tried to sort things out, she vaguely remembered Jason taking her out to her car and forcing himself on her. She was devastated and ashamed of herself for allowing herself to get caught in this situation. She didn't know what to do.

discussion questions

1. What should Ashley do?
2. Many women in this situation feel that they are at fault. In the case of date rape, who is at fault and why?
3. What, if anything, can women do to protect themselves from date rape?
4. Imagine that you are Ashley's friend (or youth pastor) and she calls you for help. What would you do? What advice would you give her?
5. What advice could you give to a friend so that she could avoid finding herself caught in a similar situation?

additional scriptures

Deuteronomy 12:28; Proverbs 27:6; 2 Corinthians 6:14; Ephesians 5:15,18; 1 Thessalonians 4:3-8

34

a driving dilemma

key verse

"Endure hardship as discipline; God is treating you as sons. For what son is not disciplined by his father?" (Hebrews 12:7).

illustration

In Jake's home state, a study was conducted that showed a dramatic decrease in accidents for newly licensed drivers when they were prevented for six months from driving with passengers under the age of 18. Most of Jake's friends are driving, and he can't wait to get his driver's license when he turns 16 in a few months.

Most of Jake's friends don't take the mandated six-month probationary period seriously. They drive their friends all around. Some of his friends do it without their parents' knowledge, while some do it with their parents' permission "as long as they drive safely." Jake's parents have told him that he is absolutely forbidden to ride in a car with anyone driving who has not already passed the six-month period. They've warned him that if he disobeys them and gets caught, he will not be allowed to get *his* license when he turns 16.

Jake thinks his parents are far too strict, and he still takes rides sometimes from his friends who are probationary drivers.

discussion questions

1. Are Jake's parent's too strict?
2. Should the fact that some of the parents of Jake's friends allow their kids to drive their friends around have any bearing on Jake's parents' decision?
3. Were Jake's parents right in imposing a consequence on him if he failed to obey their rule? Does this seem fair given the circumstances?
4. Is Jake wrong to drive with his friends?
5. As Jake's friend, what would you say to him?

additional scriptures

Deuteronomy 4:9; Ephesians 6:1; Colossians 3:20; 1 Corinthians 15:33

35

inappropriate behavior?

key verse

"But among you there must not be even a hint of sexual immorality, or of any kind of impurity, or of greed, because these are improper for God's holy people" (Ephesians 5:3).

illustration

The youth group at Valley Church was close for many reasons. The youth pastor, Seth, had invested nearly a decade among the kids, and as a result, he was able to watch many of his students grow from junior high into the college-age group. He and the present and former members of the youth group shared lots of history, experiences and growth in Christ that knit them together in devoted relationships.

One day, Seth was called into a private meeting of his ministry peers. At first, Seth thought it was just a planning meeting for the remainder of the programs in which his group and some of the other youth groups in the area were involved. However, Seth quickly discovered that this was not the case. He was devastated to find that his ministry peers had determined that his behavior among some of the students in his youth group was inappropriate.

Seth asked the leaders at the meeting what they were talking about. One pastor replied he had been receiving some complaints about Seth's actions, and that he and the other leaders had also witnessed this behavior and agreed that it was inappropriate.

When Seth asked the leaders for specifics, he was told that hugging and putting his arm around his kids was not to be tolerated. One pastor even noted that Seth had kissed one of the girls after she won a competitive event. His ministry colleagues believed that he was either flirting with the young women in his group or possibly sexually harassing them.

Seth was shocked and unable to defend his actions. For the remainder of the meeting, he sat in the back of the room near tears.

discussion questions

1. Was Seth behaving in an inappropriate manner with the kids from his youth group? What if he did the same types of actions with kids from other groups?
2. How far is too far when showing affection to another Christian?
3. What can Seth learn from this?
4. Has a youth leader ever made you feel uncomfortable? What, if anything, did you do about it?
5. What should a student do if he or she feels someone in authority is crossing the line?

additional scriptures

Psalms 7:8; 26:2-3; Proverbs 4:25-27; Romans 14:12-13; 1 Thessalonians 4:2-8

36

only one time

key verse

"Do not be deceived: God cannot be mocked. A man reaps what he sows" (Galatians 6:7).

illustration

Sarah was like any other Christian girl. She had been going to church since she was a baby and had been involved in all kinds of church activities. She had been in children's choir and youth choir. She went on mission trips and was on the student leadership team. Then came her senior year of high school.

Sarah had always liked guys who were a bit on the wild side, but she had always been able to persuade them to come to church with her. She even seemed to be a positive influence on them. Then came Ryan. Ryan was one of the most popular guys in school, and when he asked Sarah out, it began one of the most wonderful romances of her young life. They went everywhere together. Like the others, Sarah got Ryan to attend church and even to go on a youth group retreat.

During spring break, Sarah, Ryan and their friends spent the week at the beach, staying in some condos. It was a typical spring break week in which anything goes, and Sarah tried drinking and smoking marijuana. She and Ryan also had sex once during that week. Sarah thought the experience was not as good as everyone said it was supposed to be, and after a long talk on the way home, Sarah and Ryan decided not to have sex again.

A couple of months went by, and Sarah and Ryan were still having the time of their lives. They were getting ready for college, going on church youth trips and having romantic dates. During this time they had not had sex again. But one day, Sarah realized that she had missed her last two periods. She went to the store and bought a pregnancy test kit, and it turned out that she was pregnant. She couldn't believe it. She had only had sex one time! Sarah thought, *Why did this have to happen to me?*

discussion questions

1. What might Sarah be feeling? What are her choices?
2. What might Ryan feel when she tells him? What are Ryan's choices?

3. When and how should they tell their parents?
4. How should the Christians in their lives respond to their situation?
5. How does God feel about this pregnancy? Why does He allow things like this to happen?

additional scriptures

Galatians 6:1-8; James 1:12-18; 4:7-12; 1 John 1:9-10

37

passing notes

key verse

"Whatever happens, conduct yourselves in a manner worthy of the gospel of Christ" (Philippians 1:27).

illustration

Tawni loved to write notes in class. She had lots of friends, and she was always giving or receiving a note from someone. Some of the notes were quite graphic, particularly those shared between Tawni and her friend Erica.

One day when Tawni got home from school, her mother was waiting for her at the kitchen table. Tawni could tell she was in trouble—her mom had "the look"—but she didn't know why. Then her mom pulled out a folded piece of paper. Tawni could tell from the way it was folded that it was a note from her purse. She knew it was the one that Tawni and Erica had written back and forth to each other and that it contained some explicit and vulgar wording.

As her mother confronted her with the contents of the note, Tawni became defensive and angry that her mom had searched through her purse.

discussion questions

1. Was Tawni's mom right in looking through Tawni's purse?
2. Where was Tawni at fault?
3. What would have been the best way for Tawni's mom to handle the situation?
4. What advice might you give to Tawni?
5. What advice might you give to Tawni's mother?

additional scriptures

Psalm 15:1-3; 1 Corinthians 6:18-20; Ephesians 4:29-30; 1 Thessalonians 4:3-8

38

the rumor

key verse

"Anyone, then, who knows the good he ought to do and doesn't do it, sins" (James 4:17).

illustration

Katie was aware that every school has its share of potentially dangerous kids. In fact, she had always been afraid that the violence in schools she had heard so much about would eventually happen at her school. Then one day, Katie heard a rumor about a boy at her school. The rumor was that the boy was talking about imitating the shootings carried out at Columbine High in 1999 and Virginia Tech in 2007.

Katie talked with her friends about telling someone in the school office, but everyone said it would be a waste of time. Besides, they reasoned, if it were true and the boy found out who told on him, he might want revenge. It seemed that everyone Katie talked to either didn't take the threat seriously or was afraid to get involved. Katie wanted to do something about the potential problem, but she didn't know what to do.

discussion questions

1. If you were Katie, what would you do?
2. What would you say to Katie's friends?
3. Do you have any of these same fears about someone at your school?
4. What do you think are some of the reasons that students turn to violence at school?
5. What can be done to stop this violence, if anything?

additional scriptures

Proverbs 3:25-26; Isaiah 41:10-13; Ezekiel 33:1-9; 2 Timothy 1:7; Hebrews 13:6

39

unequally yoked

key verse

"Do not be yoked together with unbelievers. For what do righteousness and wickedness have in common? Or what fellowship can light have with darkness?" (2 Corinthians 6:14).

illustration

Jenna had been raised in a Christian home all her life. She thought her mom and dad were the strictest parents in the world. They had finally given her permission to date when she turned 16, but her last conversation with them had really bugged her.

A boy that Jenna liked named Jason had taken her to their high school basketball game and then to the dance after the game. He had been very polite to Jenna's parents and a gentleman toward her, and he had gotten her home right on time. The next day, however, Jenna's mom asked her if Jason was a Christian. Jenna immediately became defensive and told her mom that it was none of her business. Jenna added that while Jason might not be a Christian, he was very nice and she liked him a lot.

That evening, Jenna's mom and dad sat down with her after dinner. "We don't think you should date Jason anymore," they said. "The Bible says that Christians should not date non-Christians."

"Mom, you married Dad before he was a Christian," Jenna responded angrily, "and then he became a believer. Isn't that a double standard?"

discussion questions

1. If you were giving advice to Jenna, what would you tell her?
2. What could her parents have done better in this situation?
3. Should Jenna's parents allow her to date Jason? Why or why not?
4. How would you respond to this statement that the Bible says that Christians should not date non-Christians?
5. How would you relate 2 Corinthians 6:14 to Jenna's situation?

additional scriptures

Proverbs 12:26; 1 Corinthians 15:33; Ephesians 6:1-3; 2 Thessalonians 3:6

40

what can it hurt?

key verse

"Can a man walk on hot coals without his feet being scorched?" (Proverbs 6:28).

illustration

Kristen considered herself a good kid. She didn't smoke or drink, and she almost lived at the church. She was heavily involved in her youth group and enjoyed the activities she and her friends there did together.

One day, Scott, a cute guy from Kristen's history class, asked her to go to the homecoming dance. Kristen was absolutely elated. The only problem was that Scott was not a Christian, and Kristen had made a decision that she would not date non-Christians. However, she rationalized with herself, saying, *It's only one dance, and besides, what can it hurt? Scott is really nice; in fact, he's nicer than some of the guys in my youth group!*

At the dance, Scott was a true gentleman. Afterward, he began to call Kristen, and they talked every day on the phone for hours. Soon, they were spending every moment they could together. Kristen had a feeling that this relationship was not right, but she was having so much fun and enjoying the attention that Scott gave her that she put those feelings out of her mind.

As their relationship became serious, Kristen listened less to her conscience and more to her emotions. After many months of going out with Scott, Kristen developed some sores. When she went to the doctor, he gave her a complete physical exam. Kristen couldn't believe what her doctor was telling her—she had been infected with herpes, an incurable sexually transmitted disease.

discussion questions

1. Should Kristen have accepted Scott's initial invitation to the homecoming dance? Why or why not?
2. What could Kristen have done to prevent contracting herpes?
3. What advice would you have given Kristen early in her relationship with Scott?

4. What advice would you give her now that she has herpes?
5. Have you ever rationalized a choice like Kristen did in this story? What was the result?

additional scriptures

1 Corinthians 6:18-20; 1 Thessalonians 4:3-8; James 4:7-8; Revelation 3:14-16

41

being the minority

key verse

"Don't urge me to leave you or to turn back from you. Where you go I will go, and where you stay I will stay. Your people will be my people and your God my God" (Ruth 1:16).

illustration

For their annual weeklong work camp, the all-white youth group traveled to a Christian conference center that was frequented by nearly all African-American churches. The purpose of the experience was to share the work alongside an ethnic group that was not represented in their own community. The group believed that they could foster understanding and cooperation by tackling a project with people whom they had been taught to avoid or even fear.

The group's arrival coincided with an annual gathering of nearly 500 African-American Christians from a three-state area to celebrate their heritage and spirituality. Driving into the campground, the leaders saw that their 26 students were going to be the only whites among a sea of 500 black students. The leaders wondered how their students would respond to the situation.

The students' tasks began as soon as they climbed out of the vans. They were to assist in preparing, serving and cleaning up the lunch meal for the hundreds who were attending this one-day conference. With no introductions, they began their work.

After two hours of hard work, the students gathered at empty tables to eat lunch and talk. As they ate the delicious barbecued food, the teens confessed that they felt uncomfortable and ignored. They expressed concerns about their purpose for being there. Many wanted to leave immediately. A few were near tears.

Just then, a young African-American girl no more than seven years old came to their table and invited them to play catch. She was especially interested in one young woman's long, blond hair and wanted to touch it. She had never seen hair like that before. Within minutes, the entire youth group was well into a game of catch.

discussion questions

1. Why were the white students so discouraged?
2. Were their concerns realistic? Why or why not?
3. How does living separately from other cultures encourage racism?
4. Why did the little girl's simple request break the ice between the groups?
5. Have you been afraid of an uncomfortable situation with a different ethnic group only to find that your fears had no substance?

additional scriptures

Ruth 1:8-18; John 10:16; Romans 3:22-24; 10:12-13; Galatians 3:26-28

42

campus confrontation

key verses

"God does not show favoritism but accepts men from every nation who fear him and do what is right" (Acts 10:34-35).

illustration

The youth group of First Church often linked up with the college campus group at State University for fun activities. Pastor Eric was the leader of both groups, so the occasional united meetings made sense. During one such meeting, the whole group was eating in the outdoor campus commons area when a traveling preacher called Brother Ned began to address the people in a loud voice. At first no one paid much attention to him, but then a large crowd began to gather to listen to him.

In his remarks, Ned called cheerleaders and girls wearing jeans "whores and harlots of Satan." He referred to other nationalities as "animals and pagans who intend to dissolve the blood of the white man." He called higher education "the nonsense of the liberals."

The longer Ned spoke, the nastier and more agitated the crowd became. Students began spitting on Ned, calling him equally foul names and throwing soft drinks at him. Suddenly, a student from the school ran to the table where Pastor Eric and the mixed group of high school and college students were sitting. "You're Christians!" he screamed at them. "How can you just sit there and not do something? Do you support what this nut is saying?"

The student then walked away in disgust.

discussion questions

1. What do you think of Brother Ned's point of view?
2. What do you think about the angry accusation of the student? Was it justified?
3. What would you have done in this situation?

4. What could Pastor Eric and the students do to counteract Ned's speech?
5. Whose behavior was worse: Brother Ned's or those who spit, hit and screamed at him?

additional scriptures

Deuteronomy 10:17; John 13:34; Acts 17:26; Colossians 3:11-16

43

mistaken identity or racism?

key verse

"My friends, as believers in our Lord Jesus Christ, the Lord of glory, you must never treat people in different ways according to their outward appearance" (James 2:1, *TEV*).

illustration

Alberto was a young Hispanic man who was spending the summer working as an intern at the city hall in Los Angeles. He was an honor student and an outstanding athlete as well as a leader in his school.

One day while Alberto was walking home from work, a police car sped up to him and the police jumped out and tackled him. The police read him his rights and then arrested him for robbing a nearby liquor store. It wasn't until Alberto was brought to the police station that he was able to prove he was not the person they were looking for.

When the white police officer realized that he had made a mistake, he just shrugged and said, "Oh well, most Chicanos find themselves in trouble with the law at some time in their life. I guess it just wasn't your turn this time."

Alberto was furious.

discussion questions

1. How would you feel if you had been Alberto? What would you have done if you were in his situation?
2. Were the police justified in their treatment of Alberto given the fact that he seemed to fit the description of the robber? Why or why not?
3. Have you, or someone you know, had a similar experience? What was your reaction? How did it make you feel about yourself?
4. Have you ever made a similar mistake about someone? Have you ever judged someone by their race, ethnic background, looks, economic status or other criteria, rather than as an individual? What were the results of your misjudgment?

5. What can be done to avoid such incidents, or are such misunderstandings inevitable? What can you personally do to try to avoid misunderstanding another person on the basis of external aspects, rather than as an individual?

additional scriptures

Leviticus 19:1; 1 Samuel 16:7; Esther 3:8-15; Romans 10:12; James 2:8-9

44

subtle barriers

key verse

"Accept one another, then, just as Christ accepted you, in order to bring praise to God" (Romans 15:7).

illustration

In a small-town high school of nearly 350 students, there were only four or five students of minority races. When nonwhite visitors came to town to shop, or when a sports team with members of other races came to compete, the teens in this town were often unsure as to how to act. Without experiences with other races, many felt disadvantaged in relating to or understanding them.

The community was not particularly racist. The fact was that it was a fairly affluent area, and in this part of the country many minorities simply could not afford to live in the town or go to its schools. It was a community mostly open to others, but for economic reasons was not available to everyone.

At a youth group meeting, one leader wondered out loud how the church could promote a climate that would make other races feel comfortable. She asked if there were subtle barriers that made minorities feel discriminated against or uncomfortable. Some ideas were offered and discussed, but they either seemed too goofy or simply impossible. Finally, one student thought it might be good to contact an African-American church in a nearby community and plan to hold a combined event to help both groups get to know one another.

Calls were made, but the other group was not interested and the idea fell apart. The white students felt sad and frustrated. They were white by chance, as was their community and school system, not by choice. How could they ever bring change?

discussion questions

1. What might be some invisible barriers this church or community has put up that might discourage minorities from feeling welcome?
2. How can this youth group get to know those of other races?

3. Was the African-American church being racist in declining to share in a combined event? Explain your reasoning.
4. How bad is racism in our communities, school systems and churches?
5. What barriers to racial equality does your own church, school, town or community exhibit?

additional scriptures

Judges 11:1-11; Psalm 133:1; 1 Corinthians 11:17-18; 1 John 3:14-16

45

what's in a name?

key verse

"The nations will see your righteousness, and all kings your glory; you will be called by a new name that the mouth of the LORD will bestow" (Isaiah 62:2).

illustration

Some students from the mid-western United States made some friends with the local Indian youth at a work camp in Ontario, Canada. As the youth were hanging out together during work breaks, the Indian youth made it clear that they were not "Native Americans." They were proud to be Indians and found the other term distasteful and offensive.

After a few days, Annie, a young woman from Ohio, asked her new Indian friend, "Molly, what's your Indian name?"

Molly, who had obviously been asked this question many times, smiled and said, "Some days it's 'Sunshine.' Sometimes I go with 'Meadow Child.' But mostly, I prefer to be 'Tall Woman Who Walks Backward to Gather Water.'" Then she and her friends burst into laughter, leaving their new friends perplexed.

Later, Molly explained to the students from the Midwest that so-called Indian names were not part of her tribe's modern culture. In most ways, they were as current as any ethnic group. While they observed some meaningful customs and learned traditional dances and the stories of their people, they did not pass on the ancient customs that had become irrelevant in modern society. However, her grandparents still had names that reflected nature or some identifying family characteristic.

Confused, Annie asked Molly why movies, TV and the media in general continued to portray her people in this erroneous fashion. Molly just snickered and knowingly asked Annie who she thought wrote those kinds of movies. She clarified that if the movie was a historic portrayal, that was one thing; but if the movie treated Indians like wild, uncivilized, drunken children, it was due to Hollywood stereotyping.

Annie, her head now swimming, asked one more question: "Then how can we know what to call your ethnic group? Some say you are Native

Americans. You say you're an Indian. Some have symbolic names; you are simply Molly. How can we know what to call you, or any other ethnic group?" Molly said she had no clue.

The youth pastor, Anthony, had a thought that helped. "I was leading a work camp in the South," he said, "and as part of our program, we had a leader of the community center talk to us about race relations. During the talk, one of the students asked him if he was black or African-American. Smiling, the man said, 'My daddy was a Negro; I'm just fine with being black, but my son insists on being an African-American. The best way is to just ask us what we prefer and respect that.'"

discussion questions

1. Why do we so often treat people from other cultures differently than we treat people from our own culture?
2. Was Annie being an airhead, or was her question to Molly about her Indian name one that you might have asked?
3. What did you think about Molly's treatment of Annie's question?
4. What is your take on Anthony's comment that we should ask people what they prefer to be called? Could you ask an ethnic person his or her preference?
5. Do you think our society is becoming overly sensitive or less sensitive to the differences among us? Is it necessary to label people groups? Why or why not?

additional scriptures

Genesis 17:1-5; Ephesians 3:14-15; Colossians 3:11; Revelation 3:12

46

borrowing the car

key verse

"Guard what has been entrusted to your care. Turn away from godless chatter and the opposing ideas of what is falsely called knowledge" (1 Timothy 6:20).

illustration

Cindy was ecstatic as she stood looking at her new driver's license. She had been anticipating this moment for a long time. This was the best birthday present ever! Today was the first day that Cindy had been eligible to get her driver's license, and she had taken her driver's tests and passed. It was incredible!

"Mom, can I have the car tonight?" she asked as she proudly drove home.

"Well, I suppose you can," her mother said after giving it some consideration. "But you need to be home by nine. After all, this is a school night, you know."

That night after dinner, Cindy picked up the keys to the car and walked toward the door. "I'll be back by nine, Mom, I promise," she said over her shoulder.

"Be careful!" her mother shouted.

After picking up a few friends, Cindy headed for the mall. Everyone was excited because Cindy was the first of their friends to get a driver's license. As the group was talking and enjoying their newfound freedom, Cindy glanced to the backseat—for just a moment—to say something to one of her friends. As she did, the car drifted to the right and slammed into a car parked on the street.

Fortunately, no one was seriously hurt, but both cars were badly damaged. Cindy was afraid of what her parents might say or do.

discussion questions

1. How might Cindy's mom act toward Cindy in light of the car accident?
2. What does age have to do with maturity?
3. How does making mistakes affect the development of maturity?

4. How do we know when someone is mature enough to handle new responsibilities?
5. What will it take for Cindy's mom to trust her with the car again?

additional scriptures

Psalm 119:105; Proverbs 19:18; 1 Corinthians 13:11; James 1:2-5

47

don't blame me!

key verse

"Don't point your finger at someone else and try to pass the blame!" (Hosea 4:4, *NLT*).

illustration

Toby was extremely unruly, disrespectful and hard to control. He was always breaking things in his mom's apartment, getting into fights at school and physically abusing his mother. Although he was young, he was more than his petite mom could handle.

On several occasions social workers had to intervene in the situation with Toby and his mother. They warned Toby of his impending doom of being removed from his home by the state and placed into a setting where his behavior could be controlled. Yet Toby refused to listen. He continued acting out.

Finally, the state was forced to act. Toby cried as his things were packed up and his social services caseworker removed him from his home. Toby blamed his mother for this new and unfair punishment.

discussion questions

1. Was there any truth in Toby's claim that his mom was at least partially to be blamed for this situation? Why or why not?
2. Do you know anyone who has acted like Toby? What happened in his or her situation?
3. Have you ever been stubborn or unruly and had to pay the price for your actions? What was the result?
4. What are a few valid gripes that society has about today's youth?
5. What are some things that society often blames teenagers for that are not necessarily true?

additional scriptures

Genesis 3:9-13; Exodus 32:21-24; Matthew 25:29; Ephesians 5:15-17; Hebrews 4:13; James 4:17

48

movie mistakes

key verses

"Trust in the Lord with all your heart and lean not on your own understanding; in all your ways acknowledge him, and he will make your paths straight" (Proverbs 3:5-6).

illustration

The outdoor event for the First Church youth group had been rained out, so Ann, the church youth worker, decided at the last minute to take the kids to a bargain movie matinee. Looking over the movie choices, she told the students not to attend any movie that would be inappropriate. "PG-13 and below," she said. There were four acceptable movies out of the eight at the Cineplex, so she felt that she could trust the kids to choose one that was not controversial.

The next day, Mrs. Davis, the mother of one of the students in Ann's youth group, called and in an angry voice told Ann how disappointed she was that she had allowed her daughter to attend an R-rated movie. The mother had just returned from viewing the movie herself and quoted numerous conversations that were filled with sexual innuendoes and bad language. While there were not actual scenes of these behaviors, the discussions were too descriptive.

Ann knew that Mrs. Davis's daughter had purchased a ticket for one of the PG-13 movies. It seemed that she and her friends had left the movie they intended to watch and sneaked into another. Now Ann had to pay the price by answering to this irate parent.

discussion questions

1. Was Mrs. Davis right to be disappointed in Ann's decision?
2. What should Ann say to Mrs. Davis? Where do her responsibilities end and the teenagers' begin?
3. How can this problem be solved? What can be done to avoid a similar situation?

4. How can such an incident be destructive to the people involved?
5. How can this be turned into a learning situation for Ann, the students in the youth group and Mrs. Davis?

additional scriptures

Psalm 5:8; Proverbs 11:4; Romans 12:8; 1 Peter 4:10-11

49

more movie mistakes

key verse

"Not many of you should presume to be teachers, my brothers, because you know that we who teach will be judged more strictly" (James 3:1).

illustration

LaKeshai decided to take her church group of mostly African-American youth to see a current movie that investigated inner-city gang behavior. The movie looked at relationships, risks and the opportunities that gang members face on a daily basis. In their own community, gang activity was just beginning to be evident among teenagers, and LaKeshai feared that ignoring the reality would seem to be a message that gang life is okay. Wanting to be proactive, she let all the parents and students know what to expect so they could responsibly decide who should or should not attend.

During the week following the movie, LaKeshai was bombarded with phone calls from parents who found the whole subject distasteful. They believed that LaKeshai was introducing "gang thinking," as they called it, to their teenagers who probably would never think of joining a gang. A few parents noted that their sons and daughters would no longer be attending youth group as long as LaKeshai was leading.

discussion questions

1. Did LaKeshai make a bad decision by taking the group to see this movie? Could she have avoided this conflict in some way?
2. Are the parents being fair? Why or why not?
3. If you were a parent, what would you tell LaKeshai?
4. If you were LaKeshai, what would you tell the parents?
5. Does the fact that LaKeshai informed the parents ahead of time about the movie reduce her responsibility? Why or why not?

additional scriptures

Malachi 2:7-8; 1 Timothy 3:1-7; Titus 1:5-9; 1 Peter 3:8-14

50

a prank not taken in fun

key verse

"The Lord's servant must not quarrel; instead, he must be kind to everyone, able to teach, not resentful" (2 Timothy 2:24).

illustration

Maggie had made incredible strides at First Church during her first year of youth ministry. She had revitalized the youth group, nearly quadrupling the number of kids who were attending. Her work was still in the early stages, but she was off to a good start.

One day at a picnic by the beach, some of the kids tried to pick up Maggie, who was still in her street clothes, and throw her into the water. Struggling, and definitely not laughing, Maggie protested. The youth ignored her and began pulling her into the lake. Suddenly, Maggie began shrieking and threatened to quit her job if she was thrown in. All laughter ceased, and the kids awkwardly put her down.

Maggie continued to yell at them, completely losing it. The day was ruined.

discussion questions

1. Was Maggie's reaction justified? Was she acting like a responsible leader?
2. What do you think was going on in Maggie's mind during this episode? Could there have been a legitimate reason for her reaction?
3. Did Maggie have the right to protest, or is she just clueless about the nature of youth ministry?
4. How do you think the youth group members felt about her threatening to quit?
5. How can the group minister to her after the event? What should Maggie do now?

additional scriptures

Psalm 37:8; Proverbs 15:8; Micah 6:8; 1 Peter 2:19-21

responsibility

51

that's why we hired you!

key verses

"What you are doing is not good. You and these people who come to you will only wear yourselves out. The work is too heavy for you; you cannot handle it alone" (Exodus 18:17-18).

illustration

As the new youth leader, Connie was anxious to get to work. In her first few months, she tried to spend equal time in getting to know the kids and in planning for the future of the youth program. She had many ideas, and there were many opportunities. The only thing lacking was adult helpers.

Connie was enthusiastic as she set out to recruit advisors. She was certain that she could find several people who would be interested in partnering with her in her new ministry. The congregation was not large, but it was amply gifted. So, over the next few Sundays, Connie surveyed her church family and began making note of likely prospects for youth ministry advisors. With nearly a dozen excellent possibilities, she began making visits and calls, asking them to join her in ministering to youth.

At first those who said no had good reasons—they were newly married, or pregnant, or had a time conflict, or were taking college classes—so Connie was not too discouraged. However, when she reached the end of her list, she began to sense an underlying resistance.

She finally spoke frankly to Adam, who was a well-respected, energetic young man with a strong and active faith. When Connie approached him, she was shocked by his reply. "Look, Connie," he said, "some of the other people you've approached called me to warn me that you were going to be asking me to help you in youth ministry. The bottom line is that it's what we hired you to do. So don't bother asking."

discussion questions

1. How do you think Connie felt after hearing Adam's statement?
2. What would you have said? What would Jesus have said?

3. How should church ministry, on every level, be approached and accomplished?
4. Was Connie trying to put her workload off on others?
5. Is ministry the responsibility of the pastor alone, or is it to be shared?

additional scriptures

Exodus 23:5; Matthew 20:26-28; John 13:12-15; Romans 12:13; Galatians 6:9-10

52

always a Christian?

key verse

"All men will hate you because of me, but he who stands firm to the end will be saved" (Mark 13:13).

illustration

Ed was shocked when he heard that Tom had been beaten up in a drug deal and nearly killed. In middle school they had been best friends. They had grown up together, gone to Sunday School together, and even attended junior high youth club together. However, when Ed became a Christian, he and Tom had slowly drifted apart.

Tom's mother had called Ed and asked him to visit Tom to try to help him. When Ed entered the room at the hospital, he did not recognize his friend. Tom's face showed the results of a severe beating. He had multiple stitches and bruises as well as swelling and flecks of dried blood on his face. He greeted Ed through puffed lips.

As the conversation proceeded, Tom told Ed about his growing drug use, his involvement with crime, his downward spiral into dealing drugs and, finally, what he had done to receive such a beating. Ed was absolutely shocked at what his old pal was telling him.

"Tom," he asked, "what happened to you that you fell so far from being a Christian?"

"I'm still a Christian, Tony," Tom explained. "I was born a Christian. I was raised a Christian. What makes you think I'm not?"

discussion questions

1. How would you answer Tom's question?
2. Why might Tom believe that he is a Christian by virtue of his family background?
3. What does it mean to lead the Christian life? How will our lives be characterized if we are truly following after God?

4. What should Ed do to let Tom see God's love for him?
5. What follow-up might Ed consider in relation to Tom?

additional scriptures

Matthew 13:18-23; Luke 12:8-9; John 3:1-21; 2 Timothy 2:12-13; James 2:14-26; Revelation 3:5

53

faith crisis

key verse

"Be merciful to those who doubt" (Jude 1:22).

illustration

Justin was a good guy who came from a strong Christian family. Unlike many of his friends, he didn't drink, party or do anything wrong outside of an occasional argument with his parents. He couldn't remember a time in his life when he didn't believe in God. He loved his youth group and had volunteered to help with mission projects. Most people viewed Justin as a strong Christian.

Justin had a major problem, however, in that he was beginning to face powerful doubts about the existence of God. He felt that when he prayed nothing happened. He didn't see God answering his prayers. As he looked around the church he had attended his whole life, he began to see hypocrites in the congregation, and he questioned God's presence in their lives. At school, Justin's science teacher taught things that were completely contrary to what the Bible said, and the more he listened to his teacher, the more confused he became.

Justin began to realize that he might be going through something he had heard of called a "faith crisis." He wanted to believe, but the doubts just kept creeping in. Not wanting to upset his parents, Justin kept going to church, but he was becoming more disillusioned each time he went.

discussion questions

1. What should Justin do at this point?
2. What verses from Scripture would you share with Justin to help with his questions?
3. Is it good to struggle with doubts? Why or why not? Do having doubts indicate that something is lacking in a person's faith?
4. Have you ever struggled with doubts similar to Justin's? If so, what was the result?

5. What should you do when you feel that God is not responding to your prayers? What should you do when you can no longer sense the presence of God in your life?

additional scriptures

Psalm 19:1-2; John 20:27; Romans 1:20; Hebrews 11:1-6; James 1:5-8

54

is Christ the only way?

key verse

"Jesus answered, 'I am the way and the truth and the life. No one comes to the Father except through me'" (John 14:6).

illustration

The youth pastor had just finished delivering his talk on the uniqueness of Jesus Christ based on John 14:6. Feeling good about the depth and delivery of his talk, he dismissed the youth group for the evening with an encouraging word.

A small group of students, however, remained seated on the floor with expressions of concern on their faces. They looked nervously at one another to see who would speak for the group. Finally, one of the girls spoke up.

"We have trouble accepting some of the stuff you said tonight," she said. "You said that Jesus is the only way to God and to salvation, but we think you're being too narrow-minded. Why do you think He is the only way? What's to say that Hindus or Buddhists or Muslims aren't the ones who really are tuned in to God? For that matter, how do you know that they're not *all* right in their own way? Don't you think it's kind of arrogant to say that Christians have cornered the market on truth? Besides, maybe the only reason we're Christians in the first place is because we were born in a country where Christianity is the main religion."

The other students nodded in agreement as the girl spoke. After she had finished, they all looked at the youth pastor and waited for him to respond.

discussion questions

1. Have you ever had some of the same questions that this group of students asked?
2. Is it possible for all religions to be equally true or equally valid? Why or why not?

3. What influence does a person's culture have on what religion he or she will adopt?
4. What conclusions about other religions can you draw from what Jesus said in John 14:6?
5. Is Jesus narrow-minded? Explain your answer.

additional scriptures

John 6:66-68; Acts 16:30-31; 1 Corinthians 3:11; 1 Timothy 2:3-6; 1 John 4:14; 2:23; 5:11-12

55

the visitor

key verse

"Greater is He who is in you than he who is in the world" (1 John 4:4, *NASB*).

illustration

The founding leader of a coven of witches began visiting a church Bible study. At first, she sat in the back and respectfully listened to what the leader was saying. Then she sat closer and began asking questions. As the weeks passed, she became more involved in the group and even asked for prayer for some family needs at the closing prayer time. All the while, the woman was still leading her witchcraft group and practicing satanic rituals that the Bible clearly condemns.

discussion questions

1. As the Bible study leader, how would you confront the situation?
2. How would you react if you found out one of the members of your Bible study group was involved in some type of occultic practice?
3. What might you say to this young woman if she came to you?
4. How would you determine if she was trying to influence the Bible study or if she was truly seeking God?
5. How does the key verse in 1 John 4:4 apply to this situation?

additional scriptures

2 Kings 6:8-16; Psalm 121:7-8; Romans 8:31; 2 Thessalonians 3:3; Hebrews 4:12-13

YOU BE THE JUDGE

judge \ jəj \ **1:** to form an opinion about through careful weighing of evidence and testing of premises **2:** to sit in judgment on; try **3:** to determine or pronounce after inquiry and deliberation **4:** to hold as an opinion; guess, think.

The following situations call for the group members to make decisions as a jury would. Each of the stories is revealed to the group in steps, with each step being a bit more complicated than the last. Students vote on what the person or persons in the story should do next after each new piece of evidence is revealed. Whenever possible, ask students to back up their decisions or reasoning with Scripture.

1

the dying prisoner

part one

In Ohio, a convicted alcoholic was sentenced to four years in prison for habitually driving under the influence of alcohol. After serving his first year, he was diagnosed with a fatal liver disease. Through his lawyer, he petitioned the court to grant him a release so that he could die with his family near him and not all by himself in prison.

Discussion: Ask the group to talk about the facts as they have heard them. Would they let him out or not? Have them defend their answers. Are there any Scripture verses that back up their thoughts? Now take a vote: Will they release him or keep him in jail? Why?

part two

This man was convicted on nine counts of driving under the influence of alcohol. The courts can only speculate as to how many times he actually drove under the influence without being caught. He is 34 years old, is married and has two kids. The man has also been arrested for breaking into other people's cars to get in out of the weather when he could not locate his own car. It was also reported that he had stolen cars on various occasions to get home.

Discussion: Ask the group to consider this new information, vote again, and defend their vote.

part three

The man's wife and family are supporting his request for release. The man's wife wants him to die at home surrounded by those who love him, and she adamantly claims that he has hurt no one through his alcoholism. She maintains that he has been sober for a solid year, and she does not believe he will fall into drinking again. His children want him home in time for what will most likely be their final Christmas together.

The doctors maintain that this man will not recover and will probably die within a year.

Discussion: Have the group discuss, debate, apply Scripture and vote. They should especially consider the wife's statement that the man has hurt no one through his alcohol use. Is that statement true? Should he be released or kept in jail?

part four

Just prior to entering jail, the man risked his life to save another person's life. Details were not given about his deed, except to say that it truly was an act of heroism.

Discussion: Ask the group if this factor changes their vote. Conclude the discussion by letting the group mull through the difficult aspects of this case. Help them to see that life is rarely as cut and dry as we think. Above all, help them to see that Jesus loves this man, even though he is in jail.

2

the repentant inmate

part one

During the weekly visit to the jail, Al, a youth pastor, found himself in a fulfilling conversation with a new inmate, Stephen. Al's rule was to never ask the prisoners what their crimes had been. If they offered this information it was fine, but Al felt that asking for this information was inappropriately nosy. In the weeks that followed, Stephen became Al's favorite prisoner. He was not only open to the gospel but also bright, witty and a solid thinker. It was refreshing to Al to share his faith with someone who was so clearly seeking God. Then Stephen told Al that he was in jail for the crime of rape. This was perhaps the one crime that Al hated the most.

Discussion: Ask the group what Al should do at this point. What should he say to Stephen knowing that he is a rapist? Should he continue to minister to Stephen? Ask them how they would feel if they were Al. And what about Stephen? Does he have a right to become a Christian? What would they do in this situation?

part two

Sensing Al's discomfort, Stephen closed up, and shortly after the two said goodbye. Al was troubled by Stephen's crime, and he could not believe that his new friend had committed such a heinous crime. To Al, rape seemed to be a total violation of all that God and society held holy. It was such a life-damaging transgression. In his previous work in a crisis center, Al had talked to many women and girls who struggled with the devastating feelings caused by rape. Nothing could be more harmful to a woman's feelings of self-worth, trust or security. Al simply could not deal with this new revelation, and so he decided to never visit Stephen again.

Discussion: Discuss with the group whether Al is acting in a Christian manner. Is he giving Stephen a fair shake? Have the students keep in mind that rape is Al's personal bottom-line sin and that he has had lots of experience in counseling women and girls who were raped. Have the group members consider if each of us has a bottom line that helps us to know our personal limitations. How might Al put closure on this?

part three

Al was unable to live with his decision, and a couple of weeks later again visited Stephen in jail. The conversation during this visit did not flow as it had in the past, and Stephen quickly realized that Al was struggling. So he asked Al for permission to share his story. Al agreed and began to listen. Stephen told Al that he knew there was no excuse for the crimes he had committed. He stated that he, too, hated himself for his crimes, and he made no claim to be a poor misunderstood victim of society. Al shuddered when Stephen told him that he had raped women more than once. In fact, he had raped three women in one week.

Stephen also told Al that not long ago, he had been happily married to the dearest woman ever. She had died unexpectedly, and in his grief he had found help from his family. His mother was especially understanding of his situation, and he spent a lot of time with her. Then, suddenly, she also died. Stephen thought he was going to die as well. The two women he loved the most in the world had abruptly been taken from him with no warning. In time, he healed somewhat and was again able to face the world. Shortly after, Stephen met a new woman and fell in love. They began to discuss marriage, and Stephen actually began to consider tying the knot once again. However, soon after they became engaged, she was killed in a car accident.

Al was dumbfounded by this unbelievable story. Stephen then explained that he began to believe that women were trying to escape from him. He became insanely angry, and in his madness he raped a college woman. Then he raped another woman, and then another, all within one week's time. His behavior left an open trail for the police to follow, and he was soon arrested.

Discussion: Have the group discuss whether these facts change the way they feel about Stephen. Talk about how life must have seemed to Stephen. How should Al feel, knowing all of this? If they were on a jury, how would they deliberate at Stephen's trial? And isn't Al on trial as well in a sense? Should a Christian be more accepting and forgiving of those who commit terrible crimes?

part four

When the case was brought to court, Stephen asked for no special treatment. He only wanted the judge and jury to consider the whole story. He

told the court that he had not tried to avoid justice in any way and that he was willing to face the consequences of his behavior. Only then could he live with his crimes. However, Stephen also wanted a relationship with Jesus Christ. Al had convinced him that Jesus could forgive him and restore him. Stephen believed that jail time with the company of Christ would be beneficial to his rehabilitation.

Discussion: Have the group close out this case by deciding what justice really is. Is it an eye for an eye as the Old Testament says? Or is it forgiveness in Christ? Or is it perhaps a combination of the two? Ask the group to decide.

3

the teen murderer

part one

Troy is good looking, a promising all-county football star, and the son of a well-liked family. He is quiet but very intelligent and well regarded by his friends and teachers. In his first year of playing football, he proved to be a natural athlete and received widespread news coverage as he made great play after play. The college scouts are already talking to him, and he's only a sophomore.

Early one morning, Troy's parents called Stan, the church youth pastor, and asked him to come to their home immediately. Troy was being arrested for the murder of his girlfriend, and he had admitted to killing her.

Discussion: Given these facts, have the group discuss how this case might unfold. Since Troy has admitted his guilt, how should he be treated? Have the group consider his age as they determine his fate.

part two

When Stan went to visit Troy in jail, he found out that Troy had broken up with his girlfriend, Amber, several weeks before. She had become overly possessive and dependent on him, and she was disturbing Troy's concentration. Troy's athletic ability was going to be his ticket to college, and he flipped out when Amber continued to call him at all hours of the night. His parents were angry with him about the 3 A.M. phone calls, which awakened the whole household, and they told Troy to take care of the problem. Lacking good coping skills, Troy was in anguish over Amber's continued calls. He was not sleeping and obviously struggling internally with the pressure. He didn't know what to do to solve this conflict.

Discussion: Ask the group how these new facts play into their thinking. Is Troy now any less guilty? Are his parents somewhat responsible? And what about Amber? Does her stalking Troy lessen his guilt? Remember to have the group use Scripture to back up their reasoning whenever possible.

part three

The newspaper reporters covering this case treated Troy as if he were destined for athletic sainthood. Many of the writers continually mentioned Troy's incredible skill as an athlete and the waste of a promising career. As the weeks passed and the case dragged on, this sad loss became a strong aspect of the case. Amber's ceaseless bothering of Troy received a lot of coverage as well. The reporters seemed to excuse Troy of responsibility for the crime. At a meeting of Troy's youth group, one young woman quietly asked a pointed question: "What about all that Amber has lost?" Silently, each one considered this question.

Discussion: Ask the group what they think of these facts. Is great athletic ability a sufficient reason to lament the waste of a life? Have the papers lost perspective? And what about Amber?

part four

Troy received 30 years in a maximum-security prison for his crime. He will be nearly 50 years old when he gets out. Compassionately, his church has continued to support him while he is in prison. Numerous people write to him and remember him at Christmas and his birthday. He has become a Christian in prison and is the chaplain's assistant. He knows God's Word well and works tirelessly to introduce other inmates to Christ.

Stan, the youth pastor, still keeps in touch. Recently, Troy asked Stan if the church would allow him to return after his release. Stan assumed so, but during the long drive home, he decides that he needs to bring this up to the church's governing body. At the next meeting of the church council, Stan asks Troy's question to the leaders. Dead silence falls as each member thinks of how he or she will respond on that day when Troy, having paid his debt to society, is released and returns to his church home.

Discussion: Ask the group what the church should say to Troy. Have them put themselves into the congregation's position. Could they worship God if they were sitting next to him in church? What would be the ramifications on the church membership? Should Troy disappear and live in another community? Also, if they knew Amber, could they forgive Troy?

4

the unruly guests

opening scenario

A group that was not associated with First Church asked if it could hold its meeting at the church. Permission was given by the church, and the group assembled for a potluck dinner. The tabletops were lined with delicious food and the participants were anxious to dig in. In fact, one fellow was so hungry that he did just that—he dug into a bowl of salad with his hand, scooping a handful of salad onto his plate. Across the table in the other line, a woman took offense at this man's behavior and told him off in front of everyone.

The pastor overseeing the gathering was alerted to the problem when the police entered the fellowship room. The woman had called them after she claimed that the man had struck her. The police were there to take the man into custody.

Discussion: Ask the group to consider this evidence. Do they think it was appropriate for the woman to call the police? Should the police arrest the man? Remember to have the group back up their reasoning with Scripture whenever possible.

part two

It seems that the man did smack the woman. While the woman was telling him off, he simply gave her hand a smack.

Discussion: Ask the group if this fact changes their previous decision.

part three

The man claims that the woman who had brought the salad was moving through the line with him. She told the man that she had forgotten to bring any type of serving utensil and, with a laugh, she had reached into her salad with her hand and put her serving on her plate. She apparently told the man that if he wanted salad, he would just have to follow her lead

and grab some. So he did. That was when the other woman across the table saw him and began the confrontation.

Discussion: Note to the group that with this piece of evidence, we have established that the man was not the first to put his hand into the salad and that the salad's owner actually encouraged him to reach in. Of course, we still have the fact that the man slapped his accuser's hand. Ask the group how these new facts affect their opinion.

part four

Another witness to this heinous crime told the police that the woman who had been smacked had failed to mention that she had struck the man first. When the man put his hand into the salad bowl, she reached over as she was telling him off and slapped his hand a number of times. In fact, this witness says that the man did not smack her as much as hit her hand away to get her to quit hitting him.

Discussion: Note to the group that from this last piece of evidence, it now appears that this bizarre situation was a battle. The woman slapped his hand several times, and he in turn hit her hand away. Then, in anger, she called the police and asked them to arrest the man. Ask the group to decide who was at fault in this situation and why. If they were the police, how would they handle this situation? How could this whole mess have been avoided?

Have the group consider this final question: What kind of publicity will this bring the church? The church was just providing space for a group that had no meeting place, yet it is the church that will be named when the story is reported in the local paper. What kind of testimony of Christ will this present to the rest of the community? Should the church give groups like this the boot? Or is this an acceptable risk?

5

the disillusioned volunteers

part one

When Sam, a second-year seminarian, came to intern at Victory Community Church, he brought with him a wealth of building skills. Sam had come from a family that owned a contracting company, and he was adept at constructing buildings and making home repairs. As he described his experiences of helping the needy by offering competent repairs to their homes as a sign of Christ's love, the whole youth group became excited about the new ways they could reach out to their community.

The high school group at Victory Community Church had never been on a work camp before. Not one kid in the group had any building experience. Yet Sam assured them all that they could do far more than they ever believed. He also told them that he would love to teach them how. For the first time, the group was excited about doing missions.

Discussion: If you have ever gone on a work camp, share your experiences with the group. If not, discuss whether that would be a good way to help others. Also ask the group how the recipients might feel about having strangers travel from a distance to fix up their homes. How might they feel if they were the ones helping those individuals? Discuss some of the barriers that might be keeping your group from going on a missions work camp.

part two

Sam thought that the best plan would be for the group to visit a local building project, where affordable housing was being constructed for poor families right in their town. He called the project director and discovered that there was going to be a house raising in two weeks' time. The project director told Sam that he would be more than happy to have Sam bring the youth group over to help.

On a warm Saturday morning, 17 teenagers stepped out of church vans and walked onto a lot filled with people, lumber, tools, equipment

and the concrete block foundation of what would soon be a frame house. Sam led his group in a prayer of dedication, and then they joined the other workers. Throughout the day, the group members from Victory Community Church did nothing but pick up litter and lumber scraps. Not one excited, ready-to-work teenager was asked to swing a hammer or drive in one nail. At the day's end, the group re-entered their vans with heavy, disappointed hearts.

Discussion: Ask the group if these teenagers were expecting too much from their workday. Would they have been disappointed if they were in these teens' situation? It could be said that cleaning up trash was just as important to the project as building walls and securing beams. Given this, shouldn't the group from Victory Community Church feel good about their contributions to the work?

part three

Sam felt bad about the building project and knew that he had to help the group rebound from the disappointment. He sensed that they needed a strong mission experience to reignite the fire that had been so evident in them before they were delegated to litter detail at the worksite. So Sam began asking around and found an inner-city soup kitchen that needed helpers at their regular Sunday meal. Excitedly, Sam shared his prior soup kitchen experiences with the group. The group again caught his enthusiasm, and the following Sunday a group of 21 teenagers walked through the doors of an inner-city church and descended to its basement soup kitchen.

The kids loved the experience. They prepared food, served meals, cleaned up and played with children. Some of the members sang choruses to those who were eating, and many chatted with those who were being served. Sam felt good about bringing the kids to the soup kitchen.

As the meal came to its conclusion, one of the young women from the group came up to Sam and told him that a man had tried to coax her upstairs for sexual favors. She was shaken by his language and descriptions of sexual activity. Moments later, one of the young men from his group also came to seek comfort. An elderly man to whom he was serving coffee had verbally attacked him with a foul racial slur. Sam, realizing that the group's safety could not be assured, gathered his group together, loaded them into the vans, and left the soup kitchen.

As the group headed home in shocked silence, Sam wondered what he could do to restore a sense of mission to these young people who had now experienced two significant strikes against their missionary zeal.

Discussion: Ask the group how they feel about these incidents. What should Sam do at this point? What should he tell his students? What could they do to rectify the problems? Why do such things sometimes happen when we are helping others? Did Sam do the right thing in removing the kids from the soup kitchen? Why or why not?

part four

With two strikes against them, the youth group was understandably resistant to considering any further summer missions programs or experiences. Sam realized that he had a looming problem, so he sought God for direction. At the next youth meeting, he opened up to the kids and asked them what they, as a group, should do in response to these horrible experiences. He gently confronted the teenagers with the fact that bad experiences do not exempt the follower of Jesus from continuing to help others, and he cited various examples of this from Scripture. Sam then asked for ideas or suggestions.

One young woman named Teresa spoke up and said that before they thought of new projects they could do, the group should look at what did not work in the last two experiences. She suggested that in learning from the bad, they might be able to invent a missions project that made sense to the group. The group discussed what had gone wrong and slowly began to put together a plan for having their own soup kitchen. The kitchen would be housed in the gym of an inner-city church with whom their church had partnered in the past. The group developed security safeguards, listed appropriate norms for behavior, and even figured out the first year's menu.

From the ashes of two bad experiences came a successful food assistance program that met the ministry needs of the teenagers and the physical needs of the homeless and poor. Soon after, the same group of teenagers decided to organize their own work camp adventures. At these work camps, all participants equally shared the duties of sawing and hammering, as well as cleaning up litter.

Discussion: Ask the group if these mission programs could have come into being without the unfortunate experiences of the first two strikeouts. Why or why not? How closely involved should teens be with work camps and other service projects? Are today's teenagers responsible, capable and concerned enough to take on major work camp or food assistance projects? Ask the group how they are serving others. What could they do to assist those in the community who are in need?

INDEXES

index \in-deks\ a list (as of bibliographical information or citations to a body of literature) arranged usually in alphabetical order of some specified datum (as author, subject, or keyword).

scripture index

subject index

thanks

Special thanks to:

Jim Liebelt—Jim's writing, editing and focusing skills helped greatly with this book. Not only is Jim an excellent writer and talented editor, but he is also a wonderful friend.

Mark Simone—Mark is one of the most creative people on planet Earth. What more can be said?!

Jean Tippit—Jean's contributions to this project proved once again that she is a joy to work with and continues to be a creative and wonderful voice in the youth ministry world.

contributors

Rick Bundschuh

Karen Bosch

Mike DeVries

Tom Finley

Jenni Knowles

Jim Liebelt

Tom Patterson

Scott Rubin

Mark Simone

Jean Tippit

Jonathan Traux

Daiv Whaley